Sewing Stylish

Handbags & Totes

Chic to Unique Bags & Purses That You Can Make

Sewing Stylish
Handbags & Totes

Chic to Unique Bags & Purses That You Can Make

Choly Knight

Design Originals

an Imprint of Fox Chapel Publishing
www.d-originals.com

Expandable Retro Messenger Bag (page 97) and Pleated Evening Bag (page 103)

© 2013 by Choly Knight and Fox Chapel Publishing Company, Inc., East Petersburg, PA.

ISBN 978-1-57421-422-2

Library of Congress Cataloging-in-Publication Data

Knight, Choly.
  Sewing stylish handbags & totes : chic to unique bags and purses that you can make / Choly Knight.
     pages cm
  Includes index.
  Summary: "Bags can be functional, stylish, colorful, or whimsical. This book shows you how to sew your own one-of-a-kind bags to satisfy all your needs and tastes. Create personalized bags that range from sophisticated to indispensable. Learn the basics of bag sewing techniques, and get tips for going green with upcycled found fabrics. We demystify the bells and whistles that go into designer bags so that you can craft your own with the same flair... but not the same price! Whether you want your bag plain and simple or detailed and complex, you'll find plenty of fun options, motifs, and ideas to get you started. Sew Stylish Handbags will guide you to create a bag that just makes your life a little easier, or a truly show-stopping piece of arm candy that really puts an outfit together. So let your imagination go wild and get sewing! Discover how to make your own one-of-a-kind bags that are quirky, modern and fun! -Get step-by-step instructions for making over 50 useful & stylish bags. -Learn the basics of fabric selection, sewing techniques, tools, hardware, and supplies. -Recreate the high-end look of designer bags at a fraction of the cost. -Discover stylish motifs that will make you look like you spent hundreds on your bag. -Go green with handmade reusable bags, upcycled found fabrics, and recycled materials. -Make a Retro Messenger Bag, Collapsible Shopping Tote, Technophile Laptop Bag, On the Town Errand Bag, and many more! "-- Provided by publisher.
  ISBN 978-1-57421-422-2 (pbk.)
  1. Handbags. 2. Tote bags. I. Title. II. Title: Sewing stylish handbags and totes.
  TT667.K59 2013
  646.4'8--dc23
                            2012046490

To learn more about the other great books from Fox Chapel Publishing, or to find a retailer near you, call toll-free 800-457-9112 or visit us at *www.FoxChapelPublishing.com*.

Note to Authors: We are always looking for talented authors to write new books. Please send a brief letter describing your idea to Acquisition Editor, 1970 Broad Street, East Petersburg, PA 17520.

Printed in China
First printing

About the Author

Choly Knight is from Orlando, Florida. She has been crafting for as long as she can remember, and has drawn, painted, sculpted, and stitched everything in sight. She began sewing clothing in 1997 and has yet to put her sewing machine away. After studying studio art and earning a BA in English, she now enjoys trying to find numerous different ways to combine her passions for writing, fine art, and craft art. She created all of the designs, projects, and patterns that appear in this book. She focuses on handcrafted clothing, accessories, and other creations inspired by Japanese art, anime, and style, and specializes in cosplay (costume play) hats and hoodies. Find out more on her website: *www.cholyknight.com*.

Contents

34

41

48

53

60

65

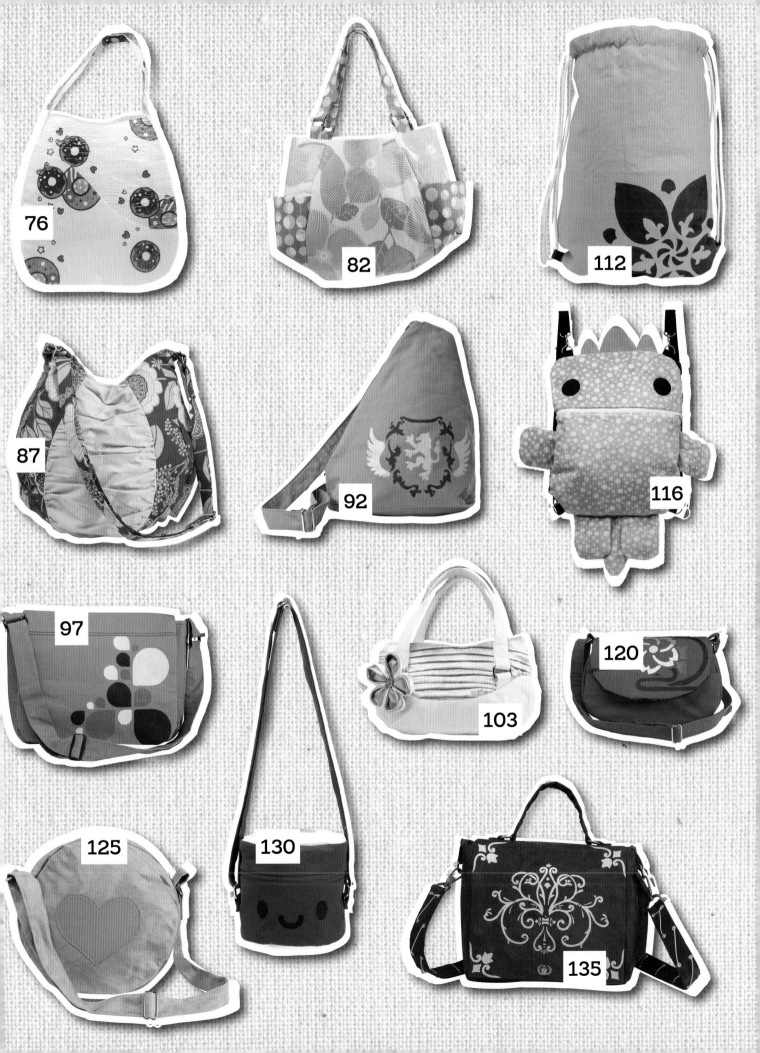

Stitch Your Way to Style!

28 Add unique appliqué pieces.

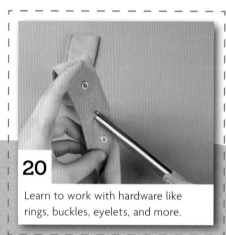

20 Learn to work with hardware like rings, buckles, eyelets, and more.

39 Learn to install zippers for purse closures and pockets.

14 Take advantage of different varieties of fabrics to get the look you want.

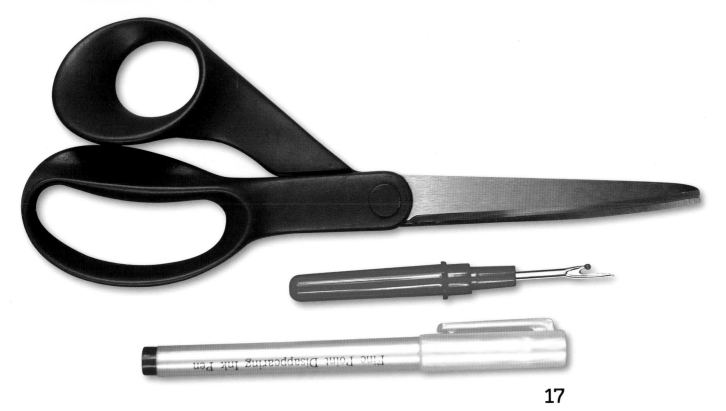

17

Build a basic sewing tool kit.

26

Understand the basic stitches.

80

Fuse plastic to create your own sewable fabric.

46

Add stenciling for a custom touch.

58

Sew on any kind of pocket you want.

107

Create custom embellishments.

Introduction

I am a self-professed bag-o-phile, bag-o-holic, bag-a-maniac, or whatever else you want to call it! I'm sure if you've picked up this book, you might be the same way. I myself prefer utility-type bags—sling bags with loads of pockets or messenger bags with zippers and flaps to hold even the smallest items. And I'm sure others lean toward luxurious designer-style handbags. I'm here to satisfy both of those cravings in this book, where I hope all my projects can get you the bag (or bags!) of your dreams.

My first real sewing project was a drawstring backpack I made at age twelve in my Home Economics class. Everything I had made before was mostly dabbling, so the prospect of making a full-fledged project excited me to no end. The pattern was very simple, yet in the end it was baffling how long it took to put together. It wasn't because I was a beginner sewer, but because my teacher had so many rules for sewing: "This fabric can't go with that," "You can't sew your seam before this," and "Your project won't look right unless you do this." It was a lot of fussiness for what, in the end, was just a simple cotton bag. I feel most crafters tend to view sewing this way: a bit of a persnickety hobby that means hours spent doing careful hand stitches with the end result of a frumpy, plain project that looks better on a thrift store shelf than in your closet.

Considering how old-fashioned sewing can be, you might not believe that by using traditional sewing methods, you can achieve some of the designer looks on department store racks. With the right techniques and attention to style, you can make your own accessories at a fraction of the cost of designer names. Unlike more conventional sewing patterns, the projects you'll find in this book have a fun and modern look. You'll see lots of ways to embellish your bags using hardware like zippers, snaps, metal rings, buckles, and eyelets. Using a little bit of elbow grease (rather than delicate and painstaking needlework), you can make a

big impact with eye-catching metal. The Mod Weekender Bag is a favorite of mine in that way, where the shape of the bag, the stenciled designs, and bold hardware are unapologetically geometric and vibrant.

And if you're willing to get your hands dirty, the wide array of stencil designs in this book can give your bags any style you like with a bit of paint and a craving for color. The same stencils can also be used for appliqué designs—and I don't mean the kind that go on your grandmother's quilts! These appliqué designs are fresh and artistic patterns that can add a whole

new dimension to your projects. You can create some really show-stopping looks with just some scrap fabric and a readiness to experiment.

I personally get a lot of my experimental inspiration from the things I'm surrounded by in my work studio. Both my computer and sewing machine are focal points in my workspace—getting down and dirty and drawing by hand is a great way to unlock my creativity, but I love the organization, efficiency, and simplicity I can get from working on my computer.

Sketching designs is a great way for me to get my creativity out on paper, but I love the streamlined efficiency of working on my computer as well!

double-duty!) to make everything efficient. My shelves reach the ceiling and every scrap of fabric I own has its place. I was sure to put that same idea into every bag I designed here; each bag has multiple charming or useful aspects, so you can use it to its fullest potential. The Reusable Shopping Tote is not only light and perfect for the grocery store, but also zips up into a tiny pouch to make it ideal for stowing away. The Reversible Creature Bag looks like an adorable stuffed animal bag, but is reversible for twice the fun! Or there's my favorite, the Expandable Retro Messenger Bag. While it has the classic messenger bag shape, it also has an array of pockets and even expands to a larger size by use of a zipper applied at the bottom. The blue trendy techno version of the bag is a nod to my love of video games. All these elements make it easy for a bag-o-phile like me to justify filling my closets with totes and purses, because each one has several defining features!

So I hope you'll enjoy adding to your bag collection from the projects here. I promise that the designs will give you plenty of bang for your buck with a minimum of old-time-sewing fussiness. I've always thought the best part of sewing is the ability to creatively express yourself exactly the way you want. I think these bags will do just the trick with all their stunning embellishments, allowing you to make the statement you desire with the beautiful accessory you've always dreamed of.

In that sense, technology motivates me deeply, whether I'm creating computer-inspired motifs, like those for the Laptop or Tablet Bag, or simply working toward designs that are more bright, modern, and bold, like those for the Roundabout Purse. I think the technology I grew up with has helped me work and see things in a streamlined way.

On the flip side, my sewing studio also has loads of books paired alongside fabrics and notions on my shelves. I love to read, and classic fantasy and science fiction stories always spark my artistic vision and help me remember to add a sense of magic and depth to everything I design. You can see this at work with the design of the Emellished Briefcase or Satchel, a luxurious faux suede bag that evokes images of distant adventures or simply writing poetry by the riverside. As I sew, I find myself viewing each piece as a canvas for more art, which helps me create appliqué and stencil designs for every project. I prefer lively, eye-catching patterns and shapes to the more mundane ribbon and trim embellishments that are usually too inconspicuous or banal to make an impact. In a sense, it's like I want each bag to have its own story to tell, and to tell it with vivacity.

Despite the array of tools I work with, I actually have a very small workspace, so you'll be happy to know you don't have to have a lot of space dedicated to your sewing to create some wonderful projects. I make sure that all of my furniture and storage work to their full capacity (if not

Choly Knight

GETTING STARTED

The projects in this book range from very easy to more intermediate skill levels, so basic sewing techniques can get you through a lot of the bags in this book. However, if you're a beginner, you might want to review this chapter to get acquainted with the fabrics, techniques, and tools you'll be using. Every technique or tool used to make a bag in this book is covered in further detail here, so whether you need a refresher or are learning these skills for the first time, you're sure to be able to create any bag you'd like with enough patience and practice.

Each project is given a level of difficulty that reflects how much time it takes to make the project and how complex the techniques are. Each chapter's projects are ranged from easiest to most difficult, so if you work your way up through the projects, you can acquire the most skills.

Super Easy: Perfect for first projects. These are quick to put together and only use a few simple techniques.

Easy: Good to tackle as a third or fourth project. Also straightforward to put together, but the techniques and time require a little more input.

Experienced Beginner: Ideal for a beginner that is through with the basics and is ready to take things to the next level.

Intermediate: For those sewers who know nearly all general sewing techniques and can easily follow a pattern with only a bit of help.

Also note that each project has several variations. These can range from different decorations and motifs that can be sewn or painted on your bag to different pattern pieces you can use to create an entirely new look. Keep an eye out for these variations when cutting out your patterns and fabric. Also keep a lookout for tips found throughout the instructions that can suggest variations to simplify or ramp up your bag.

Level: Super Easy

Level: Easy

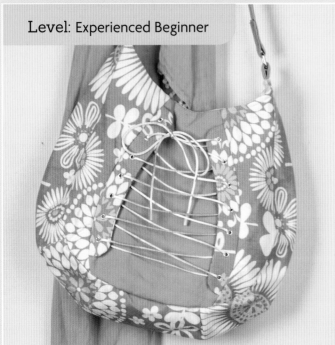

Level: Experienced Beginner

Level: Intermediate

Quilting cotton

Fabrics

The fabric you choose for your bag is essential, as it will determine how the finished product will behave and hold up to what you store in it. Be sure to keep this in mind when shopping for your fabrics. Will the bag be for special occasions and only hold keys and a wallet? If so, then lightweight fabrics such as cotton and satin will be fine. Or will the bag be used every day for holding important items, like a laptop and power cord? Heavyweight fabrics like home décor canvas and suede are better for this more frequent use. Maybe the bag will just be used casually for running errands and holding a few essentials. Medium-weight fabrics like suiting and twill are the perfect fit, and not too fussy.

With this in mind, stretchy knit fabrics such as jersey, interlock, or spandex don't work well as bag material. To determine if a fabric is too stretchy for a bag, pull about 10" (25.5cm) of the fabric horizontally. If it stretches more than a few inches, it will do the same when you fill your bag. Your items will likely pull your bag out of shape, causing it to hang uncomfortably and look odd. If the fabric only stretches an inch or so, you can usually get away with using it after applying some interfacing.

When shopping, you'll see most fabrics come in widths of 45" (114.5cm) and 60" (152.5cm). The materials list for each project will make note of this and give fabric requirements based on fabric widths, so make sure you are aware of your fabric width before deciding on the amount you'll need. If the project doesn't mention fabric width, then either width is suitable for the amount suggested.

The following are the various types of fabrics used for the projects in this book.

Lightweight fabrics

Quilting cotton

Normally reserved for quilts, quilting cotton is a versatile, lightweight, and easy-to-sew fabric with a plethora of designs and colors to choose from. It responds well to ironing, folding, and other techniques, and holds up for years despite being so lightweight.

Silk & satin

A very luxurious and eye-catching fabric, satin can be finicky to work with but is worth it for the look it achieves. It comes in various kinds of weaves that can make a big difference in sewing. Brocaded satin and dupioni are firmer and easier to work with, while charmeuse drapes nicely but is slippery and harder to keep where you want it. Using a special sewing needle for lightweight fabrics is suggested for satin and silk.

Silk & satin

Medium-weight fabrics

Corduroy & denim

Often thought of just for pants, corduroy and denim do a great job as a medium-weight fabric for bags. Keep in mind that some of these fabrics can be very stretchy, so avoid those. Also, some varieties of denim are much thicker and are better categorized as heavyweight fabrics.

Twill

Consider a pair of comfortable khaki pants, and you'll get the idea of what twill fabric is like. It's very easy to work with and bends to your will as a sewer. Because of this, the variety of colors and prints available in twill has been expanding. Thicker varieties of heavyweight twill can be found with the home décor fabrics. See more about those below.

Suiting

Suiting fabric is a bit of an umbrella term to cover fabrics that work well in making suits. They're typically made from combinations of wool, polyester, and rayon and come in sophisticated and classic colors and prints.

Suiting

Twill

Faux suede

Home décor fabrics

Heavyweight fabrics

Faux suede

A real treat for bag makers, faux suede is supple to the touch, very tough, and relatively easy to work with compared to other heavyweight fabrics. And, unlike real suede, it often comes in lots of unique colors, too. Especially thick pieces of faux suede should be sewn with sewing machine needles labeled for leather.

Home décor fabrics

Another umbrella term covering all fabrics used for interior decorating, home décor fabrics include canvas, heavyweight twill, chenille, and other fabrics for curtains, furniture, and pillows. They are especially sturdy because they are meant for upholstery and the like, but keep in mind how difficult it might be to work with some of these fabrics. They often get very thick and ornamented, so play around with the fabric and see how it feels and reacts to pulling, folding, and twisting. Consider that how it reacts at the store will be the same as how it reacts when you're ironing, folding, and sewing with your machine.

Corduroy & denim

Other fabrics

Fleece

Fleece is a plush fabric often seen in warm, lightweight jackets and stuffed animals alike. For that reason, fleece is typically only used in novelty bags like the Reversible Creature Bag, though it can also be substituted for any project that calls for a medium-weight fabric.

Vinyl & faux leather

Vinyl and faux leather are heavyweight fabrics that act more like plastic. They have great strength and durability, but are often difficult to work with because they don't run through the machine easily. A lightweight stabilizer can help with this; see the Sewing Tools section (page 17) for more information. Also be sure to use a sewing machine needle specifically for vinyl or leather when sewing with these fabrics.

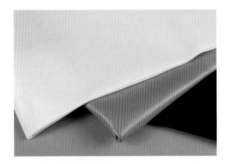

Recycled materials

Special sections in this book include how to melt and reuse plastic bags for sewing and also how to laminate items with iron-on vinyl for sewing. Anything from grocery bags, food bags, old books, artwork, and even gift wrapping paper will work! These materials will act very similarly to vinyl and faux leather and will require a needle for vinyl to sew properly.

Lining fabrics

Most of the bags in this book call for some kind of lining. While it's optional, it lends a very professional touch to your bag. Fabrics specifically for lining are very similar to a lightweight satin and can be just as slippery and tricky to work with. Quilting cotton is a great alternative for beginners.

Found fabrics

You'll find a great resource for bag-making supplies at thrift stores or anywhere else used items are sold. Old pants or jackets make for wonderfully sturdy fabric and old dresses are nice for lining and special occasion purses. Even better are the bits of old hardware you can find on old purses, belts, and carryalls. See the Handbag Hardware section (page 20) for more details.

About Metric

Throughout this book, you'll notice that every measurement is accompanied by a metric equivalent. Inches and yards are rounded off to the nearest half or whole centimeter unless precision is necessary. Please be aware that while this book will show 1 yard = 100 centimeters, the actual conversion is 1 yard = 90 centimeters, a difference of about $3^{15}/_{16}$" (10cm). Using these conversions, you will always have a little bit of extra fabric if purchasing by the metric quantity.

Sewing Tools

While basic sewing tools are more than enough to get through some of the simple projects in this book, you'll find that some more advanced tools are needed for complicated and designer looks. Here, you'll find what should be in your basic sewing kit first, and then a list of more specialty items. Look over them to see if you need to add to your sewing arsenal.

Basic sewing kit

Sewing machine: A good, reliable sewing machine with a straight and zigzag stitch can sew all of the projects in this book with ease. A presser foot with adjustable pressure is also a plus.

Sewing shears: Sharp sewing shears are essential for cutting pattern pieces from fabric, as regular scissors usually aren't sharp enough. With this in mind, use sewing shears only on fabric, as materials like paper can quickly dull them.

Craft scissors: A typical pair of comfortable scissors works fine as craft scissors. Use these to cut paper patterns or any other material that would dull sewing shears.

Tape measure or ruler: Some bags will require that you draft your own pattern pieces from given dimensions. A tape measure or ruler is crucial to get accurate cuts.

Seam ripper: This tool is essential for any sewer and makes it a breeze to correct mistakes.

Iron: Not all fabrics are well suited to ironing, particularly vinyl and similar materials, but those that are look much more polished after ironing. An iron is also essential for applying interfacing and fusible web, as discussed later.

Fabric marker or tailor's chalk: Because sewing is much like assembling a puzzle, making marks on your fabric is helpful when lining up pieces. The pattern pieces that accompany the projects will have marks that need to be transferred to the fabric for this reason. Air- and water-soluble fabric markers or washable tailor's chalk do the job best.

Sewing kit tools:
In addition to a reliable sewing machine and iron, the essential tools for every project include shears, a seam ripper, a ruler, and a fabric marker.

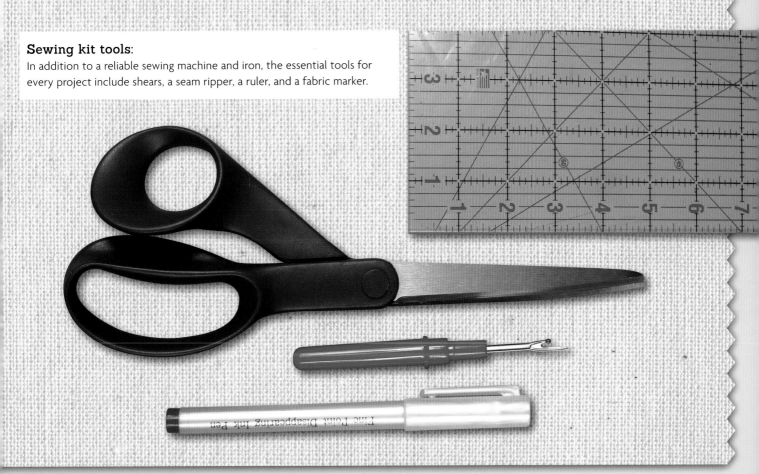

Sewing pins: A standard tool for keeping fabrics pieces together before sewing, pins come in different sizes that are suited to different weights of fabric. However, it's best to pick whatever feels most comfortable to you. Keep in mind that some fabrics, such as vinyl, should not be pinned, as the holes left by the pins are permanent.

Sewing machine needles: Universal sewing needles are a great place to start, but be aware that many heavyweight fabrics, and especially vinyl and faux leather, need needles specifically designed for those fabrics. You will also find needles designed for lightweight to medium-weight fabrics and for denim. Match up your needles closely to your fabric's weight, and replace them often (usually after every project) for the best results.

Hand-sewing needles: Most hand-sewing needles are called for to sew bits of lining. Sharps are a small needle well suited to this. However, when working with thicker fabrics it's better to select a bigger needle, such as an embroidery or tapestry needle, that can easily handle piercing thick fabrics. You may also want to invest in a thimble to help push the needle.

Thread: All-purpose thread works nicely for most fabrics, but some thicker fabrics may need thicker home décor thread. Another option is embroidery thread, which works nicely when doing appliqué, as introduced later.

Zipper foot: A zipper foot is a special attachment that may have come with your sewing machine. It's not an absolute necessity, but can make applying zippers a bit easier. For more information, see the Installing Zippers feature (page 39).

Pinking shears: If the raw edges of the fabric of your bag are exposed, those edges might start to unravel with time or washing. Most of the bags are lined, avoiding this problem, but if you are making an unlined bag, pinking shears can be used on the edges to prevent unraveling.

Rotary cutter: Like a pizza cutter for fabric, a rotary cutter is a very sharp cutting tool for quickly cutting squares of fabric. It works best when held against a ruler and on a cutting mat to prevent unwanted scratches on your work surface.

Pliers: With all the metal hardware used on purses, sometimes pliers can be handy in bending and twisting these items to your needs.

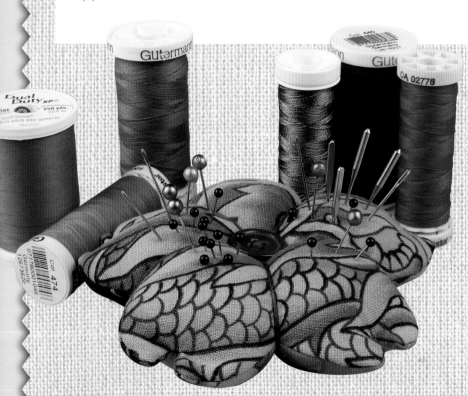

Special tools: Pinking shears, rotary cutters, pliers, and zipper feet are extra tools that might be worth adding to your arsenal.

Sewing kit supplies: Pins, needles, and thread should also be in every sewing kit, though the types of needles and thread can depend on the fabric used and your own tastes.

Additional supplies

A number of other supplies are often called for when making bags. They don't fall under tools or fabric, but can often be found with notions, embellishments, and similar products. You might already have some of these on hand, or, if you plan on making many bags, it doesn't hurt to have a surplus.

Interfacing: This material is used for stabilizing and giving greater support to fabric. It comes in iron- and sew-on varieties, as well as various weights. When attached to your bag's fabric, it will make the fabric more stable and rigid. This is perfect if you want to use a lightweight fabric for a project that would normally require a heavyweight fabric, or to eliminate any stretching that your fabric might have. Interfacing also helps your bag keep its shape when you want it to have a particular look. Interfacing is sold by the yard or in precut packages. The majority of interfacing comes in 22" (560mm)-wide widths, so the projects in this book will reflect that when listing required materials.

Fusible fleece: Similar to interfacing is fusible fleece. It is a fiber that adheres to your fabric, just like interfacing, but provides cushion as well as support. Your fabric will be rigid and keep its shape, but also be slightly padded, making it great for bags that are holding delicate items like laptops. In addition, there are also insulated varieties perfect for lunch bags. Fusible fleece also comes by the yard or in precut packages. Most fusible and insulated fleece comes in 22" (56cm)-wide widths, so the projects in this book will reflect that when listing required materials.

Fusible web: Fusible web is a paper-backed adhesive that can be ironed onto your desired fabric. Once a piece is ironed to your project, the paper is removed and the leftover adhesive can be ironed to another surface. This serves as a great substitute for sewing pins. The main use for fusible web in this book is for appliqué. Learn more about it in the Appliqué section (page 28).

Stabilizer: Stabilizer is a fibrous material that can be layered beneath your fabric to prevent complications in sewing. Fabrics such as vinyl can sometimes stick to the machine rather than glide smoothly when sewing, and using a sheet of lightweight stabilizer beneath the fabric can prevent this. Stabilizer is also a huge help in appliqué; you can find out more about it in the Appliqué section (page 28).

Hook-and-loop tape: A common choice for bag closures, hook-and-loop tape is perfect for messenger bags, lunch bags, or any kind of low-key bag in lieu of fancier hardware.

Elastic: Used in this book for making pockets, elastic adds a nice touch to roomy pockets that need to be cinched in. Thin ¼" (0.5cm) to thicker ¾" (2cm) varieties are used for the projects in this book.

Cording: Found with the webbing and ribbon in craft stores, cording comes in lots of varieties, from polyester to leather to cotton. Some bags use cording as backpack straps, while others use it for lacing through eyelets as a decorative feature, so both plain and decorative cording are used here.

Webbing: Seen often with the ribbon, webbing is the term used for woven straps used for bags. They're made from polyester or cotton and often come in a few basic colors. Webbing is a great alternative if you need a very heavy-duty strap or want to skip making one from fabric.

Ribbon: Available in grosgrain, satin, and wired varieties, ribbon is used as another decorative aspect for bags in this book.

Bias tape: Made from cloth fabric cut on the bias (for a slight, but smooth, stretch), bias tape comes in many colors and is used to bind raw edges of fabrics quickly and easily. When the folded fabric is opened, it fits snugly over the raw edge and is sewn down.

Interfacing & fusible fleece: Interfacing adds stability to fabrics and comes in light-, medium-, and heavyweight varieties. Other special interfacings are fusible fleece and insulated fleece.

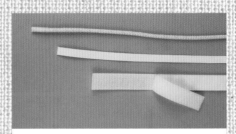

Closures by the yard: Hook-and-loop tape, elastic, and cording are notions used to close and cinch up bags.

Webbing, ribbon & bias tape: These other notions are useful both for looks and utilitarian purposes.

Handbag Hardware

If there is any one thing that sets a plain bag apart from a designer one, it would have to be the hardware. While plain or basic bags might have some webbing straps and a hook-and-loop tape closure, designer bags tend to be covered with buckles, snaps, hooks, and rings. Sometimes they're useful, and sometimes they're just for show, but they always catch your eye and have a look of importance to them. For that reason, it's easy to get intimidated by hardware, but with some patience and determination, you can achieve the same high-end look as designer handbags and totes by trying your hand at installing hardware.

You'll find most hardware materials at fabric and craft stores, usually in their own section due to the popularity of creating handbags. If they can't be found there, handbag hardware is also abundant in leather craft stores and online. However, a handy resource for these items is also your local thrift store, where you can dissect a cheap bag for all its hardware at a fraction of the cost of new supplies.

Handles

Purse handles are becoming a popular item with fabric stores, and a lot of the projects in this book can accommodate them. Available in solid plastic, bamboo, fabric, or wood varieties, they often attach to the bag via holes at each end. These holes can have rings installed, or fabric straps slipped through them and attached to the bag. The projects here will suggest purchased purse handle sizes if they can be installed on the bag.

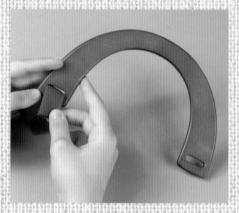

Rings

This hardware usually comes in square, circle, or semicircle shapes that add interest to how straps are attached to the bag. A fabric strap is usually slipped through each side; one strap is attached to the bag, while the other forms the handle.

Purchased handles:
Most purse handles have rings or holes at each end to make installation easy. You can slip a fabric tab through the holes, and then sew the tab to your bag.

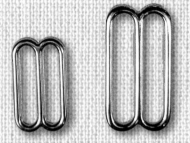

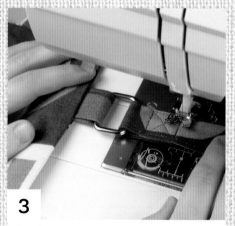

1

Insert the tab.
First, a sewn fabric tab is looped through the ring.

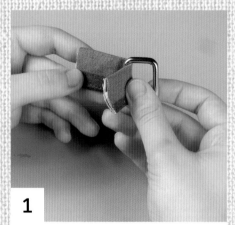

2

Apply the tab.
With the tab folded in half, baste it to your outer bag where the pattern indicates. This will hold it in place while you sew the lining.

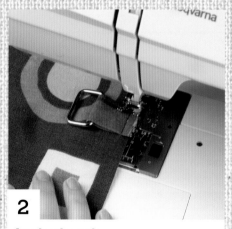

3

Apply the strap.
Your already sewn strap is applied to the other side of the ring. While the ring essentially creates an extra step while adding your bag strap, the professional look can't be denied.

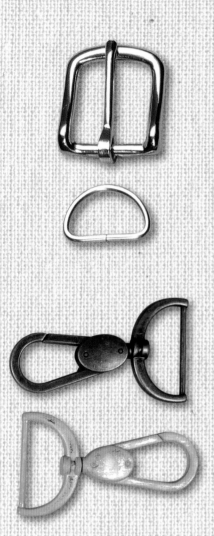

Buckles

Another kind of closure, but more complex than hook-and-loop tape, buckles are used to secure two fabric straps together temporarily. One strap is looped around the center bar of the buckle, and a small cut is made to make room for the prong to go through. Another fabric strap has eyelets installed or more holes cut for the prong. Both straps are attached to the main bag, and the strap with eyelets can then weave through the frame of the buckle.

1

Make the loop.
If you don't have a center bar buckle, this will hold down your buckle strap. Cut a ¾" (2cm)-wide strip of your fabric and fold it in thirds while sewing a medium zigzag down the center. Cut the length to three times the width of your buckle tab and sew the ends together to make a ring.

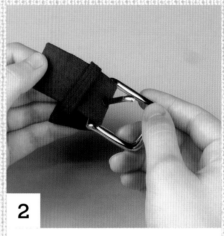

2

Insert the tab.
The tab piece from your project will indicate where a hole should be cut. The prong of the buckle goes through this hole, and the tab wraps around the bar. Slip the loop from the previous step onto the tab here.

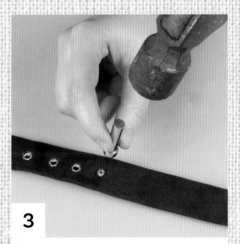

3

Prepare the strap.
Sew the strap piece as the pattern indicates, and set eyelets where the pattern markings are.

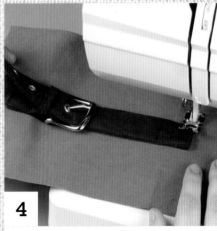

4

Apply the pieces.
Both the buckle tab and strap are applied to the main fabric with box stitches. When they are set at the right distance, the strap can weave into the buckle just like a belt, creating the finished product.

Tri-glides

Tri-glides are a type of strap adjuster made from metal or plastic and usually consist of a ring with a center bar. Installed properly, this piece of hardware can make your bag strap adjustable to fit a number of different tastes.

Zippers

Zippers are a great staple for a professional-looking bag. Small-toothed varieties are perfect for tiny, inconspicuous details, while large, metal-toothed varieties make a bold statement. Specialty zippers such as those with two heads or reversible varieties make interesting touches and can be found online if not in stores. For tips on how to install zippers, see the Installing Zippers feature (page 39).

Zippers, eyelets & snaps: These kinds of hardware are typically used as closures. They take a bit of effort to install, but are worth the professional look.

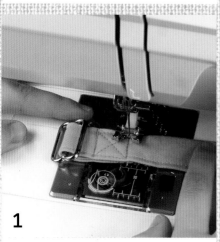

1

Sew the first end.
With your sewn strap, loop one end around the middle bar of the tri-glide, and sew it in place with a box stitch.

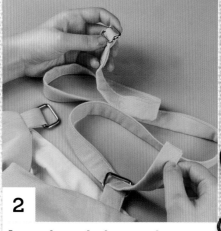

2

Loop through the metal ring.
With the other end of the strap, loop through one handle ring of the finished bag.

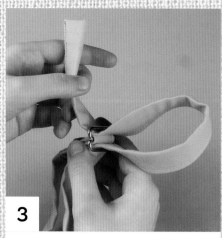

3

Loop through the tri-glide.
Continue to loop the strap up through one end of the tri-glide, then down through the other end.

4

Secure the other end.
Continue to loop the strap end through the remaining handle ring, fold it over, and secure the end with a box stitch.

Strap adjusters

Usually seen on backpacks and other utilitarian bags, strap adjusters work best with webbing. One end of the webbing is looped through the top of the strap adjuster, while the other end is looped through the bottom. It can then be pulled for tighter straps or loosened for a relaxed fit.

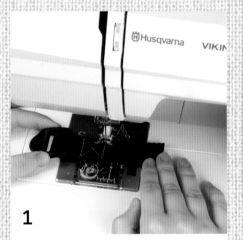

1

Sew the base end.
Cut your webbing to the length the pattern indicates. It will usually be rather short, as this is the anchor end and will not adjust. Wrap the webbing around the strap adjuster bar next to the ridged bar, fold it over, and secure it with a box stitch.

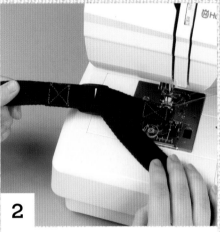

2

Sew the adjustable end.
Cut the second piece of webbing for the adjustable end. Loop this up between the strap adjuster bars, and down over the bar with the ridges. Making sure the adjustable strap is long enough, fold over the end that you slipped through the adjuster, and sew a box stitch to prevent the strap from slipping back out.

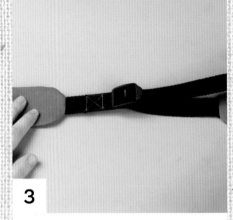

3

Install the strap.
The strap is now ready to be installed on the backpack or bag. Sew each raw end to your backpack straps and the length is now adjustable.

Hook rings

Similar to rings, hook rings have one end for a fabric strap to pass through, while the other end has a snap closure meant to loop around another ring. This lets you take off the bag handle when you desire.

1

Apply the hook ring.
Wrap your sewn strap through the opening at the top of the hook ring. Fold it over and sew it in place with a box stitch. Repeat this with the other side of the strap and another hook ring.

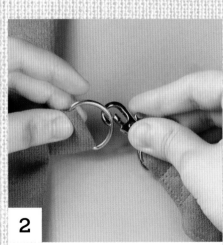

2

Install the strap.
Clip these hook rings onto the D-rings of your finished bag, and you now have a removable strap.

Turn locks & magnetic snaps

Another elegant alternative to simple closures, magnetic snaps and turn locks are particularly sophisticated and can be installed without any sophisticated tools. Fabrics with this hardware installed should be medium-weight to heavyweight, or at least have interfacing applied for stability.

1
Mark the placement.
Use the pattern guidelines to find the general area where the hardware should be placed. Press the prongs from your turn lock or magnetic snap onto the fabric to mark specifically where the prongs will go.

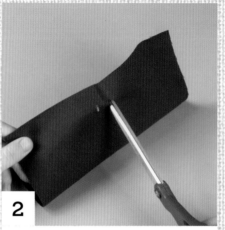

2
Cut room for the prongs.
Cut slits for the prongs where the markings were made.

3
Install the base.
Insert the prongs through the slits, and then slide the metal base over the prongs. Using pliers, bend the prongs outward to secure the hardware. This process is the same for installing the other side of a magnetic snap, so repeat Steps 1–3 with the other piece of fabric.

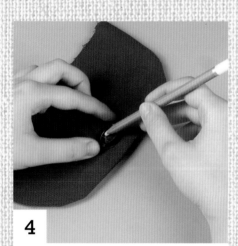

4
Mark the opening.
For a turn lock, the top piece forms an opening for the base piece to fit through. Using the top hardware piece as a guideline, mark the oval shape you need to cut for the base piece to fit through.

5
Cut the opening.
Using scissors or a craft knife, cut the oval opening based on the markings made during the previous step.

6
Install the top.
Slide the prongs of the top hardware piece through the oval opening, and then slide the top's base piece over the prongs. Like in Step 3, bend the prongs outward to secure the hardware in place.

Clothing snaps

An elegant closure compared to hook-and-loop tape, clothing snaps can be sewn onto a bag or installed with setting tools and a hammer. Fabrics with clothing snaps installed should be medium-weight to heavyweight, or at least have interfacing applied for stability.

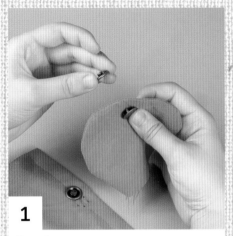

1

Set the snaps.
Metal snaps have four components and lock together with prongs once installed. Set them to your fabric according to the pattern guideline for your project. Make sure the snap pieces will align to close properly.

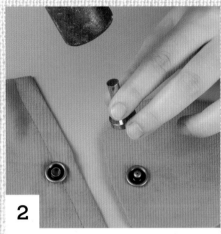

2

Install the snaps.
Use the snap setting tools to set the snaps in place.

Eyelets

Also known as grommets if they are bigger, eyelets are metal rings installed into small holes in fabric to secure the raw edges. They are used for decorative purposes on their own, or can have laces put through them. They can be used alongside buckles to create a belted look. If you are using eyelets, you will also need eyelet setting tools, which usually come with the eyelets and may require a hammer. Fabrics with eyelets installed should be medium-weight to heavyweight, or at least have interfacing applied for stability.

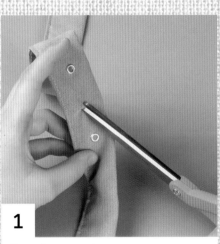

1

Cut the opening.
Use the pattern guideline to determine where the openings for your eyelets need to be cut. A small snip is fine for tiny eyelets, but larger grommets may need full holes cut from the fabric.

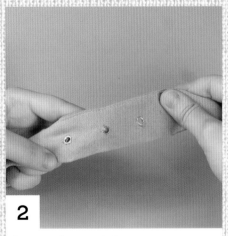

2

Insert the eyelets.
Push each eyelet through a hole. It should be a snug fit so that when the eyelet is hammered the ridges bend over the raw edges of the fabric.

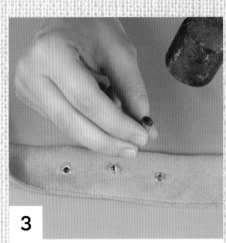

3

Install the eyelets.
Use the eyelet setting tools to either press or hammer the eyelets into place.

Basic Sewing Techniques

Most of the sewing techniques used for bags are basic ones that are familiar to any casual sewer, but if you are still new to sewing or confused by a new term or technique, this is great place to review and clear up any jargon.

Basting stitch:
A type of stitch that is meant as a temporary hold and not a true seam. It can be done by hand or by machine, depending on the intended outcome.

Basting stitch

This is a type of hand stitch made by running the needle up and down through the fabric at about ½" to 1" (1.5cm to 2.5cm) intervals. It can also easily be done by machine with the longest stitch the machine has available. This is to provide a temporary hold for the fabric until a real seam is made. The stitches can then be removed or left in place if they are sewn within the seam allowance.

Ladder stitch

A very helpful stitch for bringing two folded edges of fabric together, the ladder stitch is used here mostly in sewing closed linings in bags. It is done by tucking the needle in and out of a ⅛" to ¼" (about 0.5cm) interval in the fold of the fabric on one side and then moving onward and doing the same on the other side. Repeat this process and the thread will create a ladder effect, but disappear into the fabric when tightened.

Pattern symbols & guidelines

The symbols found all over the patterns in this book are there to help you assemble your bag accurately. Each pattern lists seam allowances, fold lines, seam lines, and grain lines. Circles indicate where an opening is left for turning the piece right side out, and gray lines are placement lines for lining up other project pieces. These can be transferred to your fabric with tailor's chalk or a fabric marker. The patterns will also tell you how many of each piece to cut and of what fabric if it helps the look of the finished bag.

Seam allowance

The seam allowance is listed on each pattern piece and indicates how much space should be between your seams and the edge of the fabric. The standard for most patterns in the U.S. is ⅝" (1.5cm), but this can vary depending on the size of the project.

Grain line

The grain line is listed on each pattern piece and indicates how the pattern piece should be laid on your fabric. To ensure the proper look, the grain line arrow should run parallel to the selvedge (the machine finished edges of the fabric), not in any other direction.

Finishing edges

In bags that don't have a lining, there will be some unfinished edges. These raw edges will fray and fall apart over time (especially with washings). Finishing the edges with pinking shears, zigzag stitches, or fray blocking liquid will prevent this.

Ladder stitch:
A hand stitch that brings together two folded edges of fabric nearly invisibly.

Finishing edges:
Raw, exposed edges of fabric should be finished with pinking shears, a zigzag stitch, or fray blocking liquid.

Hems

In bags that don't have a lining, the top edge of the bag is finished with what's called hemming. Single-fold hems are often done with pockets, while double-fold hems are usually done on the main bag. The edge of the bag is folded down twice to cover the raw edge and then sewn in place.

Clipping corners & curves

When the instructions call for clipping corners and curves, it refers to trimming or clipping the seam allowances of convex or concave corners and curves to create a smoother seam when the piece is turned right side out. Convex corners and curves should be notched or trimmed to accommodate excess fabric when the shape is inverted, while concave corners and curves should be trimmed or clipped to accommodate the fabric stretching when it is turned.

Box stitch

These are done around the ends of straps attached to your bag for added support and strength. They are done by sewing a square around the end of the bag strap and then going diagonally across the square, creating an hourglass shape within the square. A single square without the X can be done for ease, but the X gives the greatest hold. Be sure to do lots of backstitching at the beginning and end of this seam for the greatest strength.

Topstitching

This is done for decorative and strength-increasing purposes on the outside of a bag. Choose a thread that you are fine with being visible, and sew another seam about ¼" (0.5cm) from the previous seam. This creates a professional touch.

Darts

These are triangle-shaped tucks made in the fabric to create a pronounced, three-dimensional shape in the fabric piece. After the marking is transferred to the fabric, it should be folded in half to make the sides of the triangle line up, and then a seam is sewn along the line.

Gathering

Ruffles or gathers are made in fabric by sewing two lines of very long straight stitches (without backstitching) within the seam allowance of your fabric piece. Tie the threads at one end of the fabric and pull on the bobbin threads at the other end. Once the piece is gathered to the desired size, knot the bobbin threads and machine sew the edge to hold the gathers in place.

Hems:
A type of finished edge, hems are done on pockets and edges of a bag that are visible on the outside.

Clipping corners & curves:
When sewing curved shapes, the seam allowances must be clipped, notched, or trimmed so the fabric lies correctly when turned inside out.

Gathering:
Ruffles are made in fabric by pulling on the bobbin threads of two lines of long stitches until the fabric wrinkles up to the desired size.

Darts:
Darts are triangle-shaped tucks sewn into pieces of fabric, giving three-dimensional shape to what would otherwise be a flat bag.

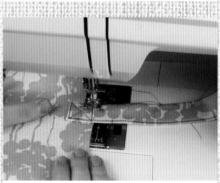

Box stitch:
A box stitch is essentially a square with an X in the middle and provides the greatest strength for attaching straps to your bag.

Appliqué

Appliqué is one of the main embellishment techniques used in this book to decorate projects. It is the process of sewing one small shape of fabric on top of another larger piece for decorative purposes. Another embellishment option is stenciling, which can be found in the Stenciling section (page 46). For machine appliqué, however, there are a few different methods that can suit your skill level, resources, or desired look.

Appliqué supplies

The simplest version of appliqué can be done with fabrics that are lighter than the base fabric, such as cotton or twill. More professional-looking appliqué can be achieved by adding fusible web and stabilizer.

Fabrics: Most every kind of fabric can be appliquéd, and a good rule of thumb is to use a fabric that is lighter than the fabric you're appliquéing on. Fabrics like cotton, flannel, and felt are a good choice, but even thinner twill, home décor, and faux suede fabrics would work well on a bag. Most of these fabrics will fray if their raw edges are exposed. That could be the look you're going for, but if not, be sure to choose your appliqué method accordingly.

Fusible web: Used in this book for appliqué, fusible web is a paper-backed adhesive. When it's ironed to almost any fabric, it makes it an iron-on patch. This patch can then be adhered and sewn to your bag with ease. It is nearly indispensible for small and lightweight appliqué pieces. However, it is optional for larger, thicker pieces of appliqué, which may only need some sewing pins to hold them in place. The lightweight variety of fusible web is ideal for appliqué and is sold by the yard or in precut packages.

Stabilizer: Often used in tandem with fusible web, stabilizer prevents warping and shifting of fabric during the appliqué process. It's very helpful for lightweight appliqué pieces and when using the satin stitch method, but is less necessary for more stable fabrics or when using the straight and zigzag stitch methods. Lightweight to medium-weight stabilizer suits appliqué best and can be found by the yard or in precut packages.

Appliqué supplies:
Appliqué can easily be done using the fabric of your choice and fusible web and stabilizer for extra support.

Appliqué techniques

Straight stitch: After applying the appliqué pieces, sew a short straight stitch about ⅛" (0.5cm) from the edge of the appliqué fabric. This will leave a raw edge, so keep this in mind when choosing the appliqué fabric (or consider using a fray blocking liquid). Lightweight stabilizer may help when sewing onto light or stretchy fabrics, but typically isn't necessary.

Zigzag stitch: After applying the appliqué pieces, sew a medium width and short length zigzag stitch over the edges of the pieces. This will leave a slightly exposed edge, which may fray or just look fuzzy with repeated use or washing, depending on how much your fabric unravels. Fray blocking liquid can be used to prevent this. Lightweight stabilizer may help when sewing onto light or stretchy fabrics, but typically isn't necessary.

Satin stitch: After applying the appliqué pieces, sew a medium to wide width and very short length (usually the shortest your machine can handle) zigzag stitch over the edge of the pieces. This takes more patience and coordination, but yields a very professional result. Medium-weight stabilizer is recommended, because the dense stitches can warp the main fabric.

This option completely encases the raw edges of the appliqué piece in thread, so there is no need to worry about unraveling. Complementary thread colors can also be used, and embroidery threads work especially well in this application, as the finished product has a beautiful sheen.

Straight stitch:
This basic appliqué method involves sewing a straight stitch close to the edge of the appliqué piece.

Zigzag stitch:
For this appliqué method, sew a medium width zigzag stitch over the perimeter of the appliqué piece.

Satin stitch:
This appliqué method uses a medium to wide width zigzag stitch at the shortest of lengths. The stitches are so close that no fabric from the appliqué piece peeks through and a professional-looking line of stitches is created.

Creating Straps

Straps are clearly what make a bag a bag, and because they are going to get so much work and stress, it's best to make them as strong and sturdy as you can. Nearly every bag in this book calls for some kind of strap or tab, so here's how to make them with ease.

Straps & handles

When these are mentioned in a project, they refer to the long rectangles of fabric meant for carrying a bag or hanging it over your shoulder. This is how handles and straps are made for the bags in this book, and you'll find in the Handbag Hardware section (page 20) all kinds of interesting bits and bobs that can be added to your finished strap.

Before you begin

Cut out all the fabric and interfacing pieces using the charts and guidelines for your project. Apply the corresponding interfacing pieces to your strap or tab pieces.

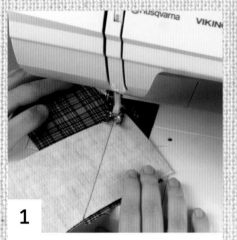

1 Join the ends.
There are times when you might not have enough fabric to make the kind of long strap that you want. To join several shorter pieces, sew along the bias while the ends are at 90° angles. Trim the seam and iron it flat for the least amount of bulk.

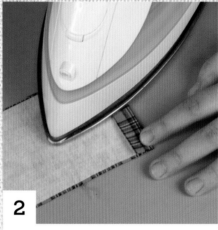

2 Fold the short ends.
Fold and iron under the short ends of your strap piece according to the seam allowance.

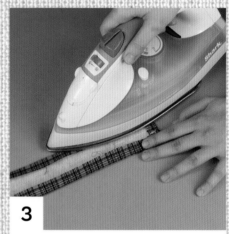

3 Fold the long edges.
Fold and iron under the long edges of your strap piece according to the seam allowance.

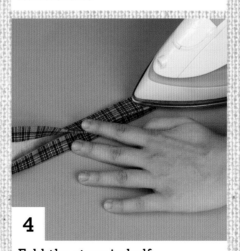

4 Fold the strap in half.
Fold the entire strap in half lengthwise and iron it. No raw edges should show.

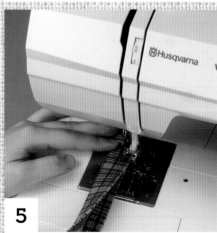

5 Sew the strap in place.
Sew the strap in place along the open edge. Your finished strap can now be sewn to your bag or any kind of hardware.

Tabs

When tabs are mentioned in a project, they refer to a shorter rectangle of fabric that is sewn into a seam of a bag. A tab is often the base for a piece of hardware, and thus encases things like metal rings

Tabs:

Tabs are created much the same as straps, except the short ends aren't turned under, but rather left raw. These ends will be sewn into the seam of the bag, so it isn't an issue.

Outer tabs

When outer tabs are mentioned in a project, they refer to a piece similar to a regular tab, but finished on all edges so it is suitable for application to the outside of a bag. The assembly is slightly different from a regular tab in order to reduce bulk.

1

Fold the long edges.

Fold and iron under the long edges of the tab according to the seam allowance for the piece.

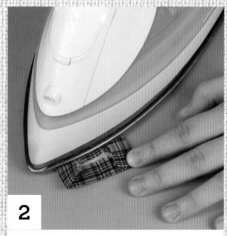

2

Fold the short ends.

Fold and iron under the short ends of the tab according to the seam allowance for the piece.

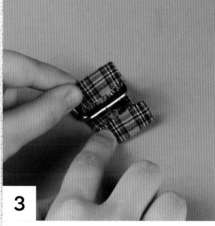

3

Fold the tab in half.

Fold the entire tab in half, looping it around a metal ring or similar hardware piece as the project dictates. The finished tab can be sewn directly onto the bag with a box stitch and is a small and inconspicuous base for the bag's hardware.

CHAPTER 1: PRACTICAL BAGS

No matter who you are, there are some bags that you just need. Regardless of eye-catching details, fancy pockets, and colorful designs, you need something that can get the job done. The bags in this chapter do just that, and with very little fuss. Here, you'll find a shopping tote, lunch bag, and even a laptop bag, all designed with functionality in mind. While it's easy to dress these up in case you'd like something with more flair, you'll find their main purpose is just to be useful and handy in both expected and unexpected ways.

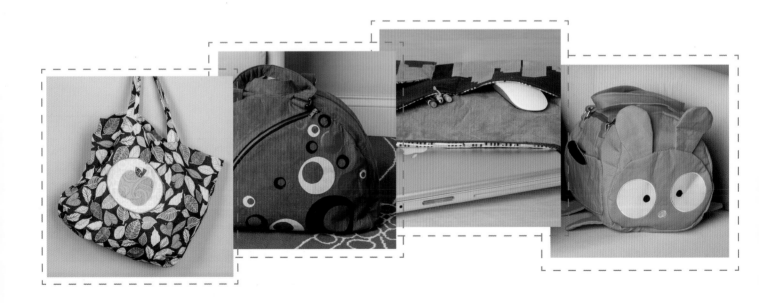

From left to right: Reusable Shopping Tote (page 34), Mod Weekender Bag (page 60), Laptop or Tablet Bag (page 41), Duffel Bags: A Three-Piece Set (page 65)

Insulated Lunch Bag, page 48

Reusable Shopping Tote

Plastic shopping bags can be very wasteful if thrown away instead of recycled, so it helps to have a reusable shopping tote like this one to use for a day of shopping. But this tote has an added bonus—a zippered wallet is built into the bag, so when it's not in use it can be zipped up easily. This way you can always carry your tote bag with you and never worry about forgetting it. The wallet section also comes with various appliqué and stencil designs to apply for a fun touch. Installing the curved zipper here might seem daunting, but the Installing Zippers feature (page 39) has a lot of helpful tips, and the techniques in the instructions keep the headaches to a minimum.

Simple Style

Classic Floral

Quirky Flair

This bag is the perfect starter project. The basic design means that even first-time sewers can complete it in minutes. Along with its simple construction, this bag is easily customizable with fun fabrics and unique appliqué or stencil designs. The attached wallet is a bonus feature that is easy to sew, but will make this bag stand out from other ordinary shopping totes.

This handy tote has an attached zipper pouch, making it easy to zip up and carry around with you for whenever you need it.

Materials

- 1¼ yd. (125cm) of 45" (114.5cm)-wide or ⅔ yd. (67cm) of 60" (152.5cm)-wide lightweight fabric
- ¼ yd. (25cm) or fat quarter contrast fabric for wallet
- ½ yd. (50cm) lightweight interfacing
- 12" (30.5cm) or longer matching zipper
- Matching thread
- Stenciling or appliqué supplies & fabric (optional)

Tools

- Basic sewing kit (see page 17)

Keep it simple

Skip the zippered wallet panel to make this a very easy project, and you've still got a fabulous tote bag!

This pattern calls for a few additional square pieces. Cut them following the chart below:

Additional Shopping Tote Pieces

PIECE NAME	MATERIAL TO CUT	SIZE TO CUT	NUMBER TO CUT	SEAM ALLOWANCE
Straps (C)	Main fabric and interfacing	3¼" x 27¼" (8.5 x 69cm)	2 of each material	⅝" (1.5cm)

See Pattern Pack for Patterns:

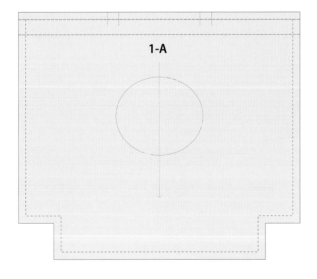
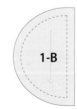

Before you begin

Cut out all the main fabric, contrast fabric, and interfacing pieces using the patterns and charts. Make any markings as indicated by the patterns. Apply the corresponding interfacing pieces to the wallet (B) and strap (C) pieces.

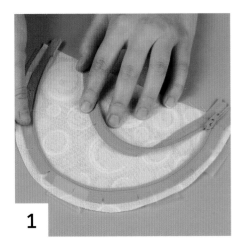

1

Apply the zipper.

Clip the tape of the zipper so it curves more easily, and apply one half of it to the curved edge on the right side of one wallet piece (B). Pin, tape, or iron it in place, using the tips from the Installing Zippers feature (page 39). Have the beginning and end of the zipper run off the ends of the curve.

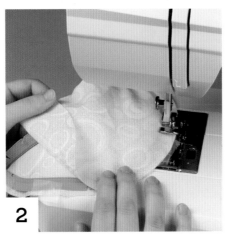

2

Sew the wallet halves.

With right sides together, layer one of the remaining wallet pieces on top of the zipper and sew the pieces together. Repeat Steps 1 and 2 with the remaining wallet pieces and the other zipper half to form the second half of the wallet. Clip the curves, turn the halves right side out, and press.

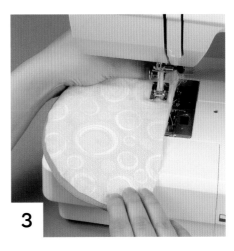

3

Sew the wallet bottom.

Move the zipper slider to the center of the zipper tape, and with the zipper facing inward, sew the bottom of the wallet, going through the zipper ends carefully but thoroughly to create the new zipper stops. Trim the excess zipper tape.

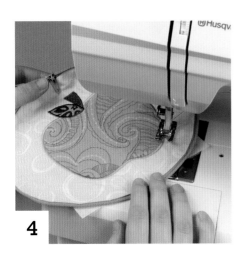

4

Appliqué or stencil.

Open out the wallet fully and either appliqué or stencil a desired image onto the outside of the wallet.

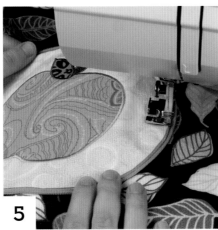

5

Apply the wallet to the tote.

Using the guidelines from the pattern, sew the wallet to the tote bag front (A) near the zipper teeth. It will be difficult to get the zipper slider to lie flat, so it's fine to skip sewing that 1" (2.5cm) space.

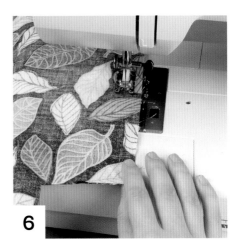

6

Sew the tote sides and bottom.

With the right sides of the bag pieces (A) facing, sew the sides and bottom of the tote, leaving the top and corners free.

7

Sew the tote corners.
Match up the side and bottom seam allowances of the tote by folding the sides at a 45° angle. Sew along the raw edges to create the corners of the tote bag.

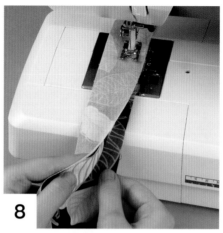

8

Sew the tote straps.
Create the tote straps (C) by sewing them in half lengthwise and turning them right side out (if using lightweight fabric) or by following the Creating Straps feature on page 30 (if using thicker fabric). Leave the short ends raw, as these will be hidden in the top hem of the tote bag.

9

Baste the straps.
Fold down the top of the tote bag (A) by ⅝" (1.5cm), and baste the strap ends to the folded edge where the pattern indicates.

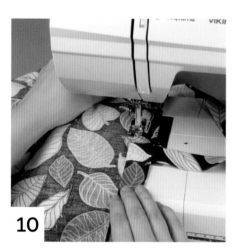

10

Hem the tote top.
Fold down an additional 1¼" (3cm) of the tote top and stitch it in place to complete the double-fold hem.

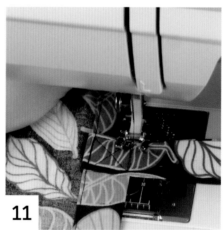

11

Box stitch the straps.
Fold the straps back upward and sew a box stitch in the area where the straps and hem overlap.

Installing Zippers

Zippers can be found on many of the projects in this book, and they add a wonderful professional look to any bag. Incorporating them into a project might seem like a daunting task, but if you view them like any other piece of fabric, you'll see that they're not so scary. Some extra tips and help here can make the process a lot less intimidating.

Zipper feet: Along with standard presser feet, most sewing machines come with some type of zipper foot. This type of foot is meant to sit snugly against the teeth of the zipper while you sew. You'll have no worries of accidentally sewing over the zipper teeth, and you'll know that the seam is even and straight. Even with this special tool, however, always sew slowly and carefully around zippers, as your sewing needle can break if it runs into the zipper slider or stop.

Pins, tape, and fusible web: Like when working with any other piece of fabric, you'll need a way to hold your zipper against your main fabric before it's sewn. Pins work well for this like with any other fabric, but items like regular tape or a thin strip of fusible web work even better for a sturdier hold.

Zipper installing supplies:
Zipper feet, pins, tape, and fusible web are helpful tools to make installing zippers an easier process.

Zipper for a purse top

This technique results in a zipper with two bag sides attached. It becomes the first step in starting a bag that has a simple, pouch-like construction.

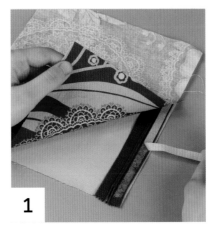

1

Prepare the zipper. Center the zipper over the edge of your fabric. With every project in this book, the zipper ends can run off the side of fabric without causing a problem. Pin, tape, or adhere the zipper to the right side of the fabric, matching up the raw edges and zipper tape. If you are using lining, sandwich the zipper between the lining and main fabric with right sides facing.

2

Start the seam. The slider of the zipper can cause an uneven seam, so slide it down before stitching a few inches into your zipper tape. Raise the presser foot and move the zipper slider back up when this is done.

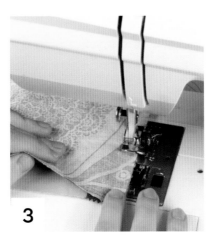

3

Finish the seam. Continue sewing toward the end of the seam, being careful around the zipper stop.

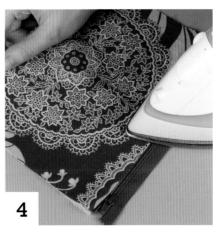

4

Fold back the fabric. Fold back the main and lining fabric from the zipper to see the completed look. Iron this lightly to avoid melting the zipper teeth and repeat steps 1–3 with the other side.

Zipper for a pocket

This is a much more detailed and difficult technique, but it is seen on a lot of designer handbags. Once you've mastered this version of zipper installation, you can use it as a patch pocket, such as the ones in the Sewing Pockets feature (page 58).

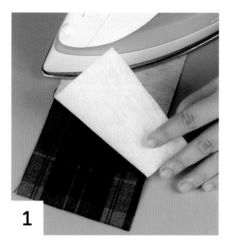

1

Interface the fabric.
Apply interfacing to the wrong side of the section of fabric that will have the zipper installed.

2

Mark the opening.
Fold under the edges of the fabric patch according to the seam allowance for the piece. Mark the outer square and inner cutting lines for the zipper on the interfacing.

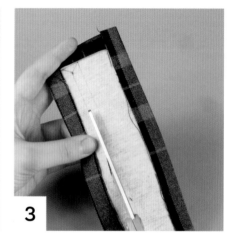

3

Cut the opening.
Cut the marked inner lines.

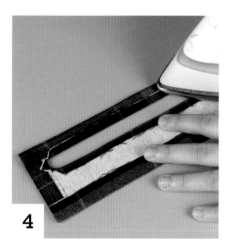

4

Open up the fabric.
Fold back the flaps made by cutting, and iron the flaps down, creating a rectangular hole for the zipper.

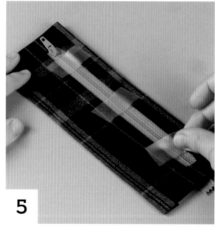

5

Place the zipper.
Center the zipper behind the opening, holding it in place with pins, tape, or fusible web.

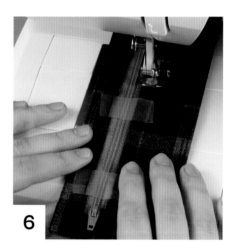

6

Sew the zipper.
From the front, sew around the perimeter of the zipper, being sure to move the zipper slider towards the middle when you get close to it. Always make sure, no matter how long the zipper may be, that the zipper slider is within the square when the seam is finished. Trim the excess zipper tape.

Laptop or Tablet Bag

Everyone with a laptop deserves a safe and sturdy bag for such a delicate piece of equipment. Sleek and stylish, this bag combines the simplicity of its basic shape with the added detail of technology-inspired motifs. The inside is lined with fusible fleece for added padding to protect all your important devices, and the outside pockets are perfect for necessities like memory cards, cell phones, or just pens and pencils. This pattern can carry large laptops with a 17" (43cm) display at dimensions of 17" x 13" (43cm x 33cm).

Sleek Modern

Trendy Two-Tone

Urban Chic

Put a twist on the classic laptop bag by adding unique pockets and stenciled designs. Use fabrics in varying shades of the same color for a neutral classic, try a two-color combination as shown above, or use a different color for each part of the bag. Switch out the technology stencil designs for flirty floral motifs or quirky characters.

Sew much more!

Have a netbook or tablet? Reduce the pattern by 50–75% of the actual size to accommodate smaller devices. Cut out the strap and tabs at the same sizes, though.

Materials

- ⅔ yd. (67cm) of 45" (114.5cm)-wide or ½ yd. (50cm) of 60" (152.5cm)-wide medium- to heavyweight fabric

- ½ yd. (50cm) of 60" (152.5cm)-wide contrasting medium- to heavyweight fabric for large pocket and strap

- ¾ yd. (75cm) of 45" (114.5cm)-wide or ⅔ yd. (67cm) of 60" (152.5cm)-wide lining fabric

- 1 yd. (100cm) medium-weight interfacing

- 1 yd. (100cm) fusible fleece

- 20" (51cm)-long zipper

- Two 1½" (4cm) metal rings

- One 1½" (4cm) tri-glide strap adjuster

- Matching thread

- Stenciling or appliqué supplies & fabric (optional)

Tools

- Basic sewing kit (see page 17)

Digital Pattern Available

Scan the code above with your smart phone or visit **http://tiny.cc/dyy3qw** to download printable patterns

Before you begin

Cut out all the main fabric, contrast fabric, lining, and interfacing pieces using the patterns and charts. Make any markings as indicated by the patterns. Apply the interfacing to the corresponding pocket (B & C), tab (D), and strap (E) pieces. Apply the fusible fleece to the corresponding main bag (A) pieces.

Switch it up!

Instead of making a strap with fabric, you can also use 60" (152.5cm) of 1½" (4cm) webbing.

This pattern calls for a few additional square pieces. Cut them following the chart below:

Additional Laptop Bag Pieces

PIECE NAME	MATERIAL TO CUT	SIZE TO CUT	NUMBER TO CUT	SEAM ALLOWANCE
Tabs (D)	Main fabric and interfacing	4¼" x 4¼" (11 x 11cm)	2 of each material	⅝" (1.5cm)
Strap (E)	Main fabric and interfacing	4¼" x 60" (11 x 152.5cm)	1 of each material	⅝" (1.5cm)

See Pattern Pack for Patterns:

(Stencil/Appliqué designs on page 45)

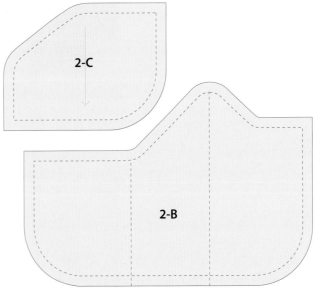

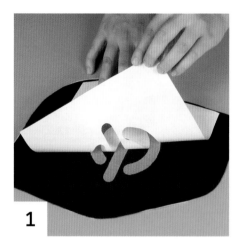

Stencil or appliqué the pockets.
Stencil or appliqué the desired designs on the large and small pockets (B & C).

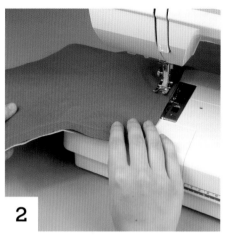

Sew the pockets
With the right sides facing, sew the lining to the outer fabric of the pockets along the upper curved edges. Leave the bottom and sides free. Clip corners and curves, turn right side out, and press.

Baste the pockets.
Line up the bottom of the pockets with the bottom of the main bag (A). Baste the large pocket (B) to the bag around the side and bottom edges. Sew the inner separations of the large pocket (B), and then baste the smaller pocket (C) in place around the sides and bottom, leaving the top free.

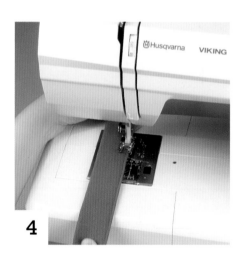

Sew the strap and tabs.
Sew the strap and tab pieces (D & E), using the method described in the Creating Straps feature (page 30).

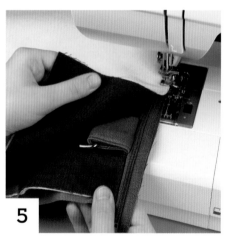

Sew the zipper.
Fold one tab (D) in half, looping it through a metal ring. Repeat with the second tab. Using the pattern guidelines, baste one tab to the left side of the main bag front and the other tab to the right side of the main bag back. With the tabs in place, layer the zipper between the main bag front and lining pieces and sew one side of the zipper. See the Installing Zippers feature on page 39 for more help. Repeat the same process for the other side of the zipper and the back of the bag.

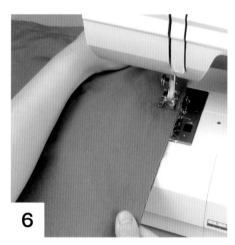

Sew the sides and bottom.
Unzip the zipper halfway and match up the two lining pieces and the two outer bag pieces with each other, right sides facing. Sew entirely around the lining pieces and then the outer bag pieces, keeping an opening in the lining where the pattern indicates for turning right side out. Sew carefully over the zipper teeth. Turn the bag right side out and sew the lining closed.

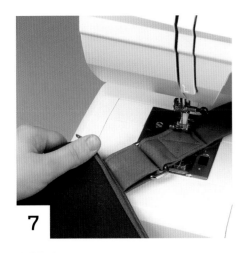

Add the strap.
Attach one end of the strap (E) to the tri-glide using a box stitch. Then loop the other end through one of the metal rings, back through the tri-glide, and through the remaining metal ring. Fold the strap end over and secure it with a box stitch. See the Handbag Hardware section (page 20) for more help.

Items for stenciling or appliqué

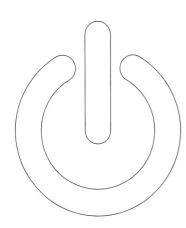

Power Symbol Motif
Copy at 200%

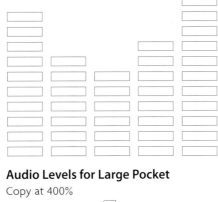

Audio Levels for Large Pocket
Copy at 400%

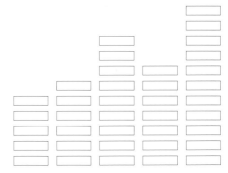

Audio Levels for Small Pocket
Copy at 400%

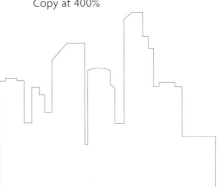

Cityscape for Large Pocket
Copy at 400%

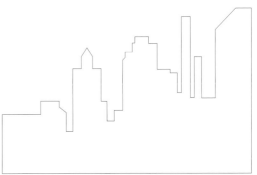

Cityscape for Small Pocket
Copy at 400%

Stenciling

While appliqué is a great way to add all kinds of designs and motifs to your work, stenciling is a wonderful option when sewing is more difficult. Using fabric paint and freezer paper, you can paint motifs where sewing might otherwise be impossible or impractical. You'll find the process a lot easier when working with fabrics that are harder to sew, such as faux suede and the like, but also with shapes that are smaller and more detailed. A few basic supplies that can be found at many craft and grocery stores are all you need.

Fabric paint: Paint specifically labeled and intended for fabric works best when stenciling. It is designed to absorb into the fabric and maintain its color through many washings. Acrylic paint also works, but you'll find that fabric paint dries much softer and feels nicer. Be sure to read the manufacturer's instructions when using the paint so that it sets properly.

Freezer paper: Originally used for wrapping food before aluminum foil and cling wrap became household standards, freezer paper is lightly coated with plastic on one side and irons beautifully onto fabric. After ironing, it sticks extremely well until you peel it off. No residue is left behind, making it like a sticky note for fabric. This makes it perfect for cutting stencils. If you can't find freezer paper at your local discount super store, it can usually be found at smaller, local grocery stores.

Brushes: When applying paint to your fabric, about any brush will do, but foam brushes tend to work the best. They apply a thick coating of paint with little agitation, perfect for getting the color down without fear of shifting the stencil.

Blades & scissors: When cutting the stencil from your freezer paper, scissors work fine until you have to cut the smaller details. Craft blades can give you better precision and make cutting intricate shapes much easier. Be very careful with craft blades, however, as they are much sharper than scissors and can easily cut your finger.

1

Cut the stencil.
Get a copy of your stencil design on regular paper. Tape it to a larger sheet of freezer paper, and, with the plastic side down, cut the stencil design through both layers with scissors or a craft knife.

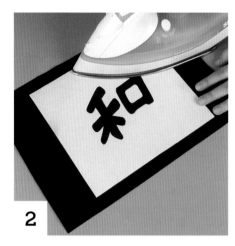

2

Iron the stencil.
Place the freezer paper stencil where you would like it on your fabric. With the plastic side down, iron the stencil firmly all over to make sure every part adheres.

3

Paint the stencil.
Place a sheet of newspaper or scrap paper underneath the fabric, as the paint might bleed through. Using an even coating of paint, paint the inside of the stencil with fabric paint. Try to use a dabbing downward motion rather than a side to side motion, as this might wedge paint underneath the stencil.

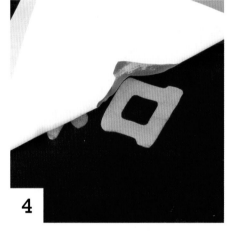

4

Remove the stencil.
Before the paint dries, peel the stencil off carefully to avoid smudging the paint. Allow it to dry thoroughly, and save the stencil for reuse if desired. Follow the manufacturer's instructions to set the paint after it has dried.

Insulated Lunch Bag

There are so many good reasons to pack your lunch for work rather than buying out, and this helpful bag will be another reason why. It's roomy enough for all the great foods you'll be stashing away, including a water bottle. The top features a wide handle for easy carrying, but then folds down when the bag needs to squeeze into a small space or isn't in use. And if that isn't enough, there's also an added pocket for a napkin that can be embellished with your choice of appliqué and stencil designs.

Classy Polka Dots

Contemporary Colors

Coffeehouse Classic

With this design, your fifth grade lunch bag is all grown up. The insulated fleece keeps your lunchtime goodies cool and fresh, while the neutral colors create a sophisticated, stylish look that's perfect for the office fridge. For a funky snack bag, use bright colors and geometric appliqué. Personalize your bag with an appliqué letter, and get excited about packing your lunch!

The front pocket of this bag is a great storage space for small items like a napkin or silverware and is perfect for an appliqué design.

Materials

- ½ yd. (50cm) of light- to medium-weight fabric
- ½ yd. (50cm) of lining fabric
- ¾ yd. (75cm) of medium-weight interfacing
- ¾ yd. (75cm) of insulated fleece
- 2" (5cm) of hook-and-loop tape
- 1½ yd. (150cm) bias tape
- Matching thread
- Stenciling or appliqué supplies & fabric (optional)

Tools

- Basic sewing kit (see page 17)

This pattern calls for a few additional square pieces. Cut them following the chart below:

Additional Lunch Bag Pieces

PIECE NAME	MATERIAL TO CUT	SIZE TO CUT	NUMBER TO CUT	SEAM ALLOWANCE
Sides (C)	Main fabric, interfacing, insulated fleece, and lining	6¼" x 15¼" (16 x 38.5cm)	2 of each material	⅝" (1.5cm)
Outer Tab (D)	Main fabric and interfacing	3¾" x 6¼" (9.5 x 16cm)	1 of each material	⅝" (1.5cm)

See Pattern Pack for Patterns:

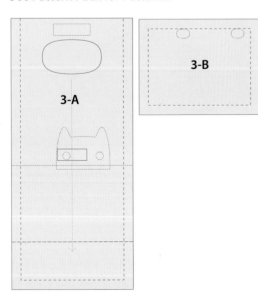

Before you begin

Cut out all the main fabric, lining, and interfacing pieces using the patterns and charts. Make any markings as indicated by the patterns. Apply the interfacing pieces to the corresponding bag front (A), side (C), and outer tab (D) pieces.

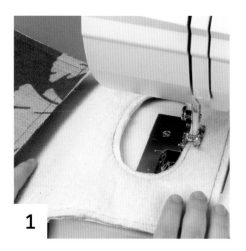

Apply the insulated fleece.
Baste the insulated fleece pieces to the corresponding main bag front, back (A), and side (C) pieces.

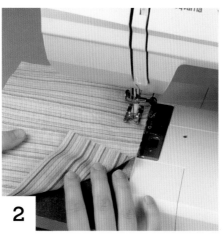

Sew the pocket.
With right sides facing, sew the pocket (B) to its corresponding lining piece along the long top edge.

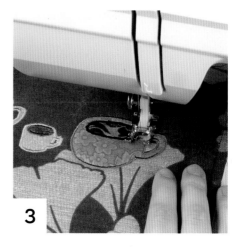

Stencil or appliqué.
Stencil or appliqué the desired designs on the front of the bag (A) and the pocket (B).

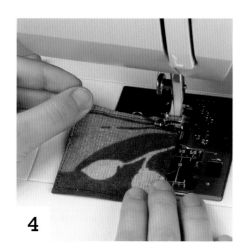

Sew the tab.
Sew the outer tab (D) using the same method described in the Creating Straps feature (see page 30).

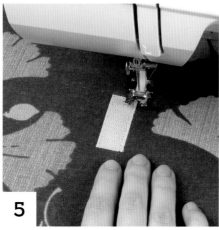

Attach the hook-and-loop tape.
Cut a 2" (5cm)-long piece of hook-and-loop tape and sew it to the back of the bag (A) where the pattern indicates. Apply the corresponding piece against one side of the outer tab piece.

Attach the pocket.
With right sides together, line the bottom of the pocket (B) up near the bottom of the bag front (A) using the pattern guideline. Sew in place and flip the pocket up so the right side faces out.

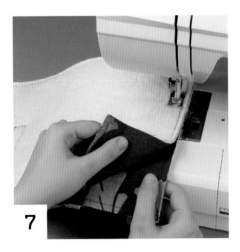

Sew the bag bottom seam.
Sew the bag front and back together along the short bottom seam.

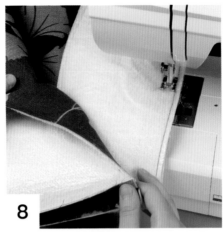

Sew the bag sides.
Sew the bag sides (C) to the bag front. Line up the upper edges, and the sides should extend ⅝" (1.5cm) beyond the bottom of the bag pocket. Sew along this long edge, stopping ⅝" (1.5cm) before the end of the side piece. Repeat this to attach the sides to the back of the bag.

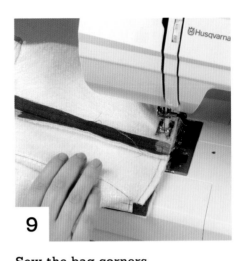

Sew the bag corners.
Line up the corners of the bag and sew across. Create the lining by repeating Steps 7–9 with the lining pieces.

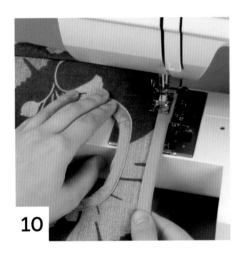

Bind the raw edges.
Wrap the bias binding around the edges of the handles and top edges and sew the binding in place.

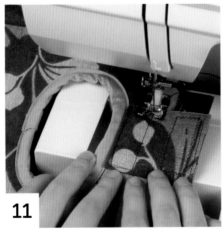

Attach the tab.
Sew the outer tab (D) to the bag front where the pattern indicates, with the exposed hook-and-loop tape facing the back of the bag.

Art & Craft Tote

This oversized clutch was created with knitters, crocheters, scrapbookers, and even artists in mind—anyone who can benefit from a portfolio-style bag meant for carrying and organizing lots of little items. When the stylish buckles are undone, the portfolio opens out like a book, displaying a plethora of pockets to hold pens, brushes, needles, scissors, findings, and lots of other tools. Meanwhile, there's an added slot for holding a sketchbook or pattern book. Use the pattern suggestions to build a wealth of pockets or use the Sewing Pockets feature on page 58 to make some of your own.

Collegiate Chic   *Flirty Print*   *Sophisticated Plaid*

Turn an ordinary artist's portfolio into an extraordinary fashion piece with academic elegance. Textured fabrics in neutral colors are perfect for a modern look, while colorful prints allow your creativity to run wild. Try a solid color for the outer bag and a colorful lining for the perfect mix of dignified and playful.

Materials

- ½ yd. (50cm) of medium- to heavyweight main fabric

- 1 yd. (100cm) of 45" (114.5cm)-wide or ⅔ yd. (67cm) of 60" (152.5cm)-wide medium- to heavyweight contrast fabric

- 1¼ yd. (125cm) heavyweight interfacing or peltex

- 1¼ yd. (125cm) medium-weight interfacing

- 1 yd. (100cm) of 45" (114.5cm)-wide or ⅔ yd. (67cm) of 60" (152.5cm)-wide lining fabric

- Four 1" (2.5cm) buckles

- Twenty ¼" (0.5cm) eyelets (optional)

- 16" (40.5cm) of ¾" (2cm)-wide elastic

- 14" (35.5cm)-long zipper

- 7" (18cm)-long zipper

- Matching thread

Tools

- Basic sewing kit (see page 17)

- Eyelet setting tools (optional)

Before you begin

Cut out all the main fabric, contrast fabric, lining, and interfacing pieces using the patterns and charts. Make any markings as indicated by the patterns. Apply the corresponding medium-weight interfacing pieces to the contrast patches (C), long zippered pocket (E), small zippered pocket (I), buckle strap (J), and buckle tab (K). Apply the corresponding heavyweight interfacing (or peltex) pieces to the front and back (A), and handles (B).

A Note on Peltex

While any heavy interfacing will do, peltex interfacing is recommended for this project. It's an extremely stiff fusible interfacing that gives the bag a stable body. It's so thick and strong, in fact, that it's easier to work with for this project when it's cut to be about ⅛" (0.5cm) within the seam allowances. Just generously cut the seam allowances off your pattern pieces after cutting your fabric and use them again to cut the peltex.

See Pattern Pack for Patterns:

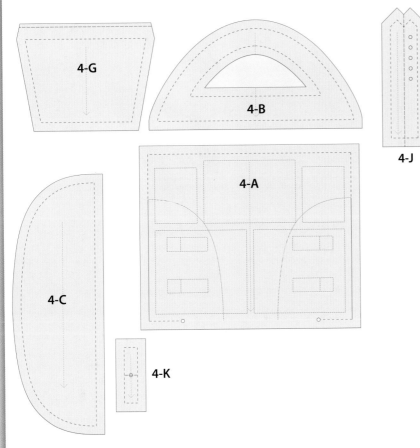
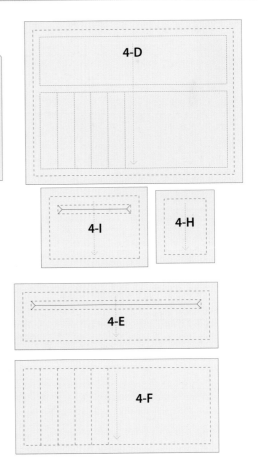

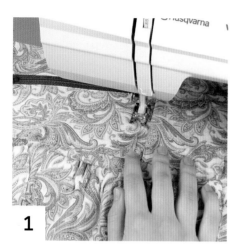

1

Apply the pockets.
Following the procedures from the Sewing Pockets feature (page 58), prepare each zippered, flat, and elasticized pocket (E–H). Use a piece of 8" (20.5cm) elastic for each elasticized pocket (G). Only finish the top edge of pocket D. Apply pockets E and F to pocket D, and pockets G–I to one lining piece (A) following the pattern guidelines.

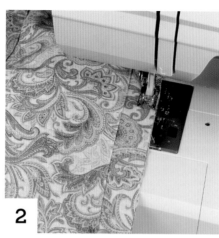

2

Baste the large pocket.
Baste the large pocket (D) to the remaining lining piece (A) along the bottom edge, creating the large pocket.

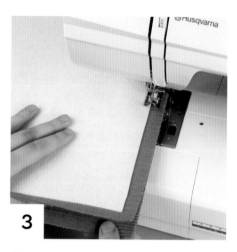

3

Sew the bottom seam.
With right sides facing, sew the main front and back pieces (A) together along the bottom seam. Do the same with the lining pieces with all the applied pockets, but leave an opening in the center as the pattern indicates for turning the bag later.

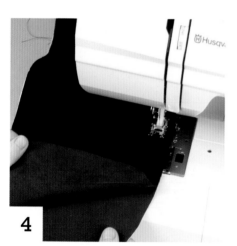

4

Sew the contrast patches.
Sew the contrast patches (C) together along the curved edge, leaving the straight edge open for turning right side out. Notch the curves, turn right side out, and press.

5

Apply the contrast patches.
Pin the contrast patches to the main bag front and back (A), lining them up with the pattern guidelines. Topstitch the patches in place.

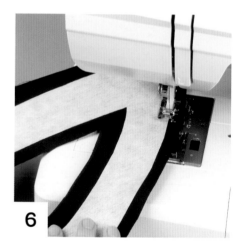

6

Sew the handle.
Sew the handle pieces (B) together along the top curved edge, leaving the bottom free for turning right side out. Notch the curves and turn the handles right side out.

7

Topstitch the handles.
Clip the opening of the handle and turn under the fabric by ⅝" (1.5cm). Topstitch this area together.

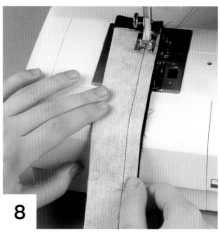

8

Sew the straps.
Turn under ⅝" (1.5cm) on each straight short side of the strap pieces (J). Do not do this with the pointed ends. Sew the straps in half lengthwise to make long tubes. Trim the seam allowance to ¼" (0.5cm), turn them inside out, press, and topstitch along the edge. Also create the buckle tabs (K) just like the outer tabs from the Creating Straps feature (page 30).

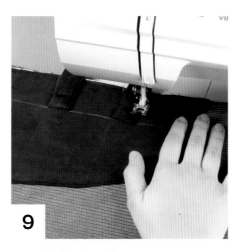

9

Install the buckles.
Use the buckle tabs (K) to assemble the buckles and apply them to the bag front (A) where the pattern indicates, using a box stitch. Apply the buckle straps (J) to the bag back where the pattern indicates, using a box stitch again. See the Handbag Hardware feature (page 20) for help creating the buckles.

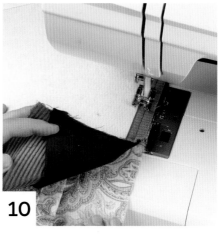

10

Complete the bag.
With right sides facing, pin the lining section to the main front and back (A). Center the handles (B) between these layers along each top edge and sew all the layers together. Clip the corners, turn the bag right side out from the opening in the lining section, and use a ladder stitch to sew the opening closed.

Sewing Pockets

Whether decorative or functional, pockets can always add to the look of a bag. On the outside they add a real look of importance, while on the inside they make organizing so much easier. In this book, mainly patch pockets are used, although there are many ways to dress up such a simple idea. This section will show you how to construct a simple patch pocket so you know exactly what to do when a pattern mentions it.

Basic patch pocket

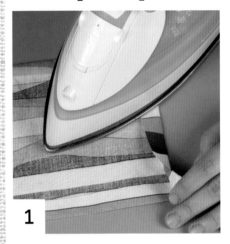

1

Fold and iron the sides and bottom.

Using the seam allowance indicated by the pattern, fold down the sides and bottom of the patch pocket and iron the creases firmly.

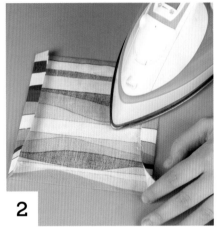

2

Fold and iron the top.

Fold the top over using the seam allowance indicated by the pattern. Iron the crease firmly.

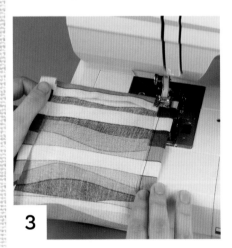

3

Hem the top.

Sew along the top edge of the pocket to hold down the fold that was made during Step 2.

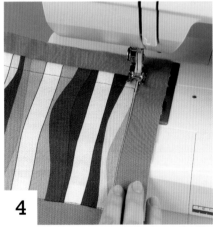

4

Sew the pocket to the bag.

Sew along the sides and bottom of the pocket very closely to the edges (about ⅛" [0.5cm]). Leave the top open and you have a finished pocket!

Deep pocket

This style of pocket has some dimension to it, making it better for holding larger items.

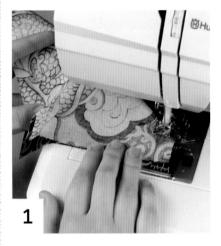

1

Sew the pocket corners.

Fold the pocket at a 45° angle so that the corners meet up. Sew along this corner to create the third dimension to the pocket.

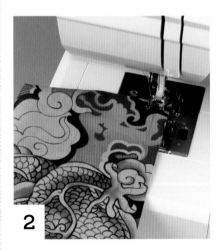

2

Finish the pocket.

Iron the sides and hem the top of the pocket as before with the basic patch pocket. Sew the sides and bottom to your bag, following the pattern guidelines, and you have a finished pocket.

Pocket flap

Sometimes it's helpful to add a flap to a pocket to help secure the items inside. Flaps can have an added snap or piece of hook-and-loop tape.

Prepare the pocket.
Prepare one of the previously mentioned pockets. Before applying it to the bag, sew hook-and-loop tape or a snap to the center where it's indicated by the pattern. After this, the pocket can be applied to the bag following the pattern guidelines.

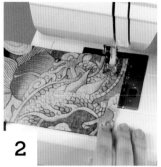

Sew the flap sides.
With right sides facing, sew around the sides and bottom of the flap piece, leaving the top open for turning right side out. Clip the corners, turn the flap right side out, and iron it. Attach the corresponding hook-and-loop tape or snap where the pattern indicates.

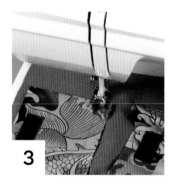

Sew the flap above the pocket.
After sewing the pocket in place, sew the flap in place where the pattern indicates above the top edge of the pocket.

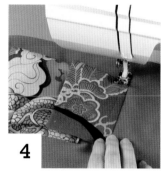

Topstitch the flap.
Fold down the flap and topstitch about ⅜" (1cm) away from the top edge of the flap. This will hold the flap in place.

Elasticized pocket

This is a variation of the deep pocket where the top is cinched in with elastic.

Hem the top.
Fold the top of the pocket where the pattern indicates to create the double-fold hem. The first fold is typically small, while the second is large enough to accommodate the elastic.

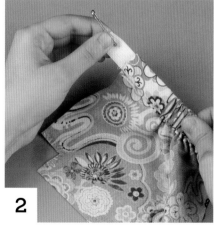

Thread the elastic.
Using a safety pin, thread the elastic through the casing made by the hem. Anchor each end with basting stitches to keep the elastic in place.

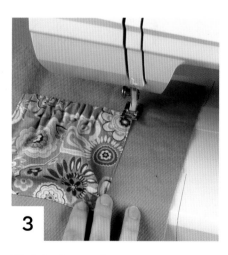

Finish the pocket.
The pocket can then be completed using the same method as the deep pocket: sewing the corners, finishing the sides and bottom, then sewing it to the bag.

Mod Weekender Bag

This bag has a timeless shape that's the perfect size for carrying enough for an overnight or weekend getaway. The inside has a helpful inner pocket, while the outside has a smart curved zipper ideal for stuffing in last-minute items like keys or plane tickets. It comes with various mod- and retro-themed motifs that go well with its classic and distinctive shape.

Dreamy Metallics

Fashion Fusion

Mod Design

The variations of this trendy bag are done in solid-color fabrics with colorful stencil designs. You can reverse this effect by using a print or textured fabric with solid-color appliqué or stencils. Don't forget to pick a fun lining for the front pocket for an extra bit of flair.

Materials

- 1⅔ yd. (167cm) of 45" (114.5cm)-wide or 1 yd. (100cm) of 60" (152.5cm)-wide medium- to heavyweight fabric

- 1½ yd. (150cm) of 45" (114.5cm)-wide or 1¼ yd. (125cm) of 60" (152.5cm)-wide lining fabric

- 2¼ yd. (225cm) of medium- to heavyweight interfacing

- 24" (61cm)-long zipper

- 20" (51cm)-long zipper

- 4 yd. (400cm) bias tape

- Four 1½" (4cm) metal rings

- Matching thread

- Stenciling or appliqué supplies & fabric (optional)

Tools

- Basic sewing kit (see page 17)

Before you begin

Cut out all the main fabric, contrast fabric, lining, and interfacing pieces using the patterns and charts. Make any markings as indicated by the patterns. Apply the corresponding interfacing pieces to the main bag back (A), pocket top (B), pocket bottom (C), bag top (D), sides (E), bottom (F), straps (G), and tabs (H).

Switch it up!

Instead of making your own handles, you can use purchased purse handles. Go for flexible ones that are at least 20" (51cm) long or solid ones that are 7" (18cm) wide.

This pattern calls for a few additional square pieces. Cut them following the chart below:

Additional Weekender Bag Pieces

PIECE NAME	MATERIAL TO CUT	SIZE TO CUT	NUMBER TO CUT	SEAM ALLOWANCE
Bag Top (D)	Main fabric, interfacing, and lining	23" x 4⅜" (58.5 x 11cm)	2 of each material	⅝" (1.5cm)
Bag Sides (E)	Main fabric, interfacing, and lining	10¼" x 8¼" (26 x 21cm)	2 of each material	⅝" (1.5cm)
Bag Bottom (F)	Main fabric, interfacing, and lining	21¾" x 8¼" (55 x 21cm)	1 of each material	⅝" (1.5cm)
Straps (G)	Main fabric and interfacing	21¼" x 4¼" (54 x 11cm)	2 of each material	⅝" (1.5cm)
Tabs (H)	Main fabric and interfacing	4¼" x 4¼" (11 x 11cm)	4 of each material	⅝" (1.5cm)
Inner Pocket (I)	Lining	12¼" x 9¼" (31 x 23.5cm)	1	⅝" (1.5cm)

See Pattern Pack for Patterns:

(Stencil/Appliqué designs on page 64)

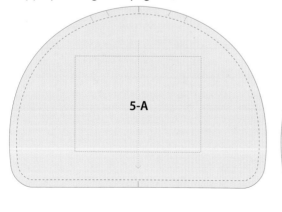

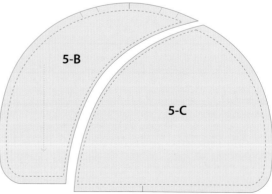

Create the pocket.
Stencil or appliqué the pocket bottom section (C) with the desired design. Clip the 20" (51cm) zipper tape so it curves easily and apply it to the edge of the pocket bottom where it will connect to the pocket top. Layer the lining on top and sew the zipper in place (see the Installing Zippers feature on page 39). Repeat with the corresponding edge of the pocket top (B).

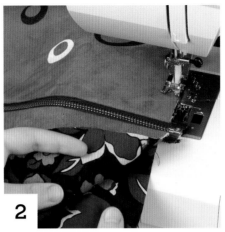

Baste the pocket to the front.
Baste the zippered pocket (B & C) of the bag to one of the lining pieces (A) all around the perimeter. Be sure to move the zipper slider toward the middle and out of the way.

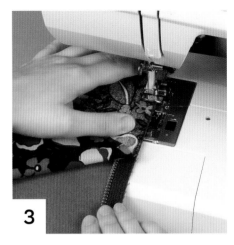

Install the zipper.
Apply the 24" (61cm) zipper to the bag top (D) and layer the corresponding lining over it. Sew the layers together and repeat with the other side of the zipper. Press the fabric away from the zipper. See the Installing Zippers feature (page 39) for more help.

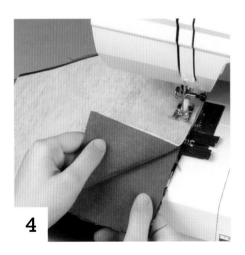

Attach the sides.
Layer a bag side piece (E) in the main fabric on top of the bag top end and place a lining piece underneath. Sew along the edge, being careful while going through the zipper. Repeat this with the other end and trim the excess zipper tape. Press the fabric away from the seam.

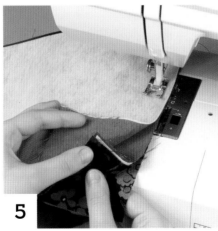

Attach the bottom.
Layer the bag bottom piece (F) in the main fabric over the end of the bag side and place a lining piece underneath. Sew along the edge and repeat on the other side with the other end of the bottom piece. Turn right side out and press.

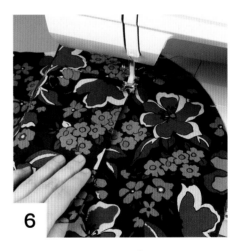

Apply the inner pocket.
Apply the inner pocket (I) following the basic pocket method of the Sewing Pockets feature (page 58). Apply it to the lining piece (A) for the bag back where the pattern indicates.

Sew the handle and tabs.

Sew the handles (G) and tabs (H) according to the Creating Straps feature (page 30).

Attach the front and back.

Find the middle of the bag top (D) and match it up with the middle of the bag front (A). Layer the bag front with its corresponding lining piece with right sides facing out, and pin them along the perimeter of the ring made by the bag top and sides. Fold the tabs (H) in half, wrapping them around the metal rings, and insert them where the pattern indicates. Notice that the tabs will be at an angle so that they point upward when turned. Sew along the perimeter. Repeat this for the back.

Finish the bag.

Sew bias tape around the raw edge between the bag sides (D–F) and front (A) to bind it. Loop the straps (G) through the metal rings secured to the tabs (H) in the top seam. Use a box stitch to sew the straps in place.

Items for stenciling or appliqué

Copy at 400%

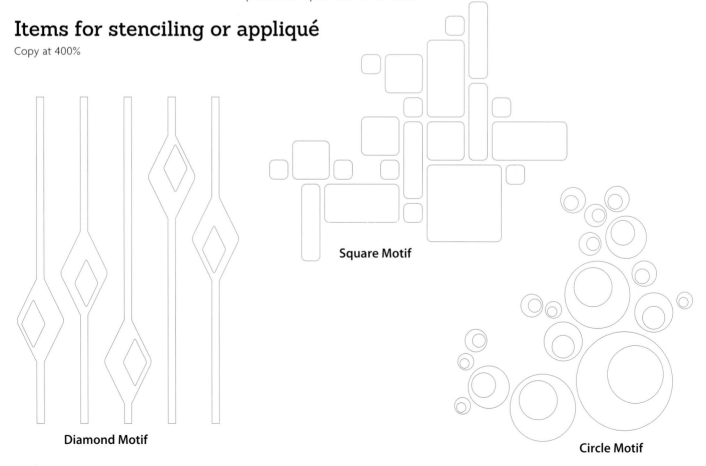

Diamond Motif

Square Motif

Circle Motif

Duffel Bags: A Three-Piece Set

You can save yourself the hassle of buying expensive luggage and be ready to travel anywhere with this set of duffel bags. With just one pattern, you can shrink and enlarge the bags just the right amount to make three different sizes. When the bags are empty, they fit snugly within each other to make storage a breeze. Each bag features lots of useful pockets on the outside and a double zipper opening on top to make it easy to reach all of your belongings. The pocket designs with vinyl tabs offer a sporty look that goes equally well with sophisticated fabrics and the included animal variations. There are patterns to make an adorable panda, cat, or rabbit, perfect for kids and kids at heart who love to travel!

Sophisticated Print

Cuddly Critters

This project presents the perfect opportunity to design your own custom set of luggage. The three bags in the set can all be made using the same fabric, or you can pick coordinating prints or colors to give each bag its own look. For a chic style, select sophisticated prints or neutral colors. If you're looking for something a bit more lighthearted, go for bright, bold colors, or turn each bag into a cute critter to travel with you.

Materials

For large bag:

- 1½ yd. (150cm) of 45" (114.5cm)-wide or 1 yd. (100cm) of 60" (152.5cm)-wide main fabric

- ⅓ yd. (33cm) of contrast fabric for pocket

- 2½ yd. (250cm) interfacing

- 1¼ yd. (125cm) of 45" (114.5cm)-wide or 1 yd. (100cm) of 60" (152.5cm)-wide lining fabric

- Two 24" (61cm)-long zippers

- 2½ yd. (250cm) bias tape

For large panda bag:

- 1½ yd. (150cm) of 45" (114.5cm)-wide or 1¼ yd. (125cm) of 60" (152.5cm)-wide main fabric

- ½ yd. (50cm) contrast fabric

- 3 yd. (300cm) interfacing

- 1⅓ yd. (133cm) of 45" (114.5cm)-wide or 1 yd. (100cm) of 60" (152.5cm)-wide lining fabric

- Two 24" (61cm)-long zippers

- 2½ yd. (250cm) bias tape

For medium bag:

- 1¼ yd. (125cm) of 45" (114.5cm)-wide or 1 yd. (100cm) of 60" (152.5cm)-wide main fabric

- 2 yd. (200cm) interfacing

- 1 yd. (100cm) of 45" (114.5cm)-wide or ⅔ yd. (67cm) of 60" (152.5cm)-wide lining fabric

- Two 20" (51cm)-long zippers

- 2 yd. (200cm) bias tape

For medium kitty bag:

- 1½ yd. (150cm) of 45" (114.5cm)-wide or 1¼ yd. (125cm) of 60" (152.5cm)-wide main fabric

- 2⅓ yd. (233cm) interfacing

- 1 yd. (100cm) of 45" (114.5cm)-wide or ⅔ yd. (67cm) of 60" (152.5cm)-wide lining fabric

- Two 20" (51cm)-long zippers

- 2 yd. (200cm) bias tape

For small bag:

- ¾ yd. (75cm) of 45" (114.5cm)-wide or ½ yd. (50cm) of 60" (152.5cm)-wide main fabric

- 1⅓ yd. (133cm) interfacing

- ⅔ yd. (67cm) of 45" (114.5cm)-wide or ½ yd. (50cm) of 60" (152.5cm)-wide lining fabric

- Two 16" (40.5cm)-long zippers

- 1½ yd. (150cm) bias tape

For small bunny bag:

- 1 yd. (100cm) of 45" (114.5cm)-wide or ⅔ yd. (67cm) of 60" (152.5cm)-wide main fabric

- 1½ yd. (150cm) interfacing

- ⅔ yd. (67cm) of 45" (114.5cm)-wide or ½ yd. (50cm) of 60" (152.5cm)-wide lining fabric

- Two 16" (40.5cm)-long zippers

- 1½ yd. (150cm) bias tape

For all bags:

- Four 1" (2.5cm) metal rings

- 10" (25.5cm) hook-and-loop tape

- 6" x 6" (15 x 15cm) remnant of vinyl

- Matching thread

- Stenciling or appliqué fabric & supplies (optional)

Tools

- Basic sewing kit (see page 17)

Switch it up!

Instead of sewing your own fabric handles, you can also use purchased handles. Be sure if they're flexible that they are at least 20" (510mm) long, and if they are solid, 8" (205mm) wide.

Before you begin

Cut out all the main fabric, contrast fabric, lining, and interfacing pieces using the patterns and charts. Make any markings as indicated by the patterns. Apply the interfacing to the corresponding main bag (A & I–L), pocket (C, D, or F), optional animal (O–U), outer tab (N), and strap (M) pieces.

This pattern calls for a few additional square pieces. Cut them following the chart below:

Additional Duffel Bag Pieces

PIECE NAME	MATERIAL TO CUT	SIZE TO CUT	NUMBER TO CUT	SEAM ALLOWANCE
Bag Top (I)				
Large	Main fabric, interfacing, and lining	6½" x 21¼" (16.5 x 54cm)	1 of each material	⅝" (1.5cm)
Medium		6½" x 17¼" (16.5 x 44cm)		
Small		5½" x 13¼" (14 x 33.5cm)		
Bag Sides (J)				
Large	Main fabric, interfacing, and lining	14⅛" x 21¼" (36 x 54cm)	2 of each material	⅝" (1.5cm)
Medium		10⅞" x 17¼" (27.5 x 44cm)		
Small		8" x 13¼" (20.5 x 33.5cm)		
Bag Bottom (K)				
Large	Main fabric, interfacing, and lining	11¼" x 21¼" (28.5 x 54cm)	1 of each material	⅝" (1.5cm)
Medium		10¼" x 17¼" (26 x 44cm)		
Small		8¼" x 13¼" (21 x 33.5cm)		
Flap (L)				
Large and medium	Main fabric and interfacing	7¼" x 3¼" (18.5 x 8.5cm)	2 of each material	⅝" (1.5cm)
Small		6¼" x 3¼" (16 x 8.5cm)		
Straps (M)				
Large, medium, and small	Main fabric and interfacing	21¼" x 3¼" (54 x 8.5cm)	2 of each material	⅝" (1.5cm)
Outer Tabs (N)				
Large, medium, and small	Main fabric and interfacing	2¼" x 3¼" (6 x 8.5cm)	4 of each material	⅝" (1.5cm)

See Pattern Pack for Patterns:

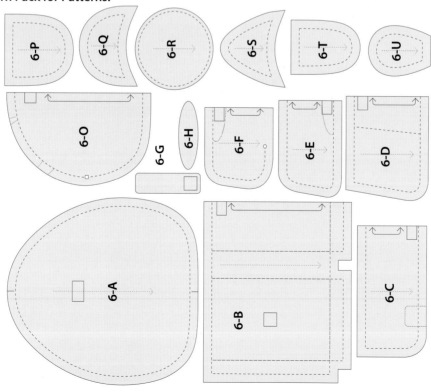

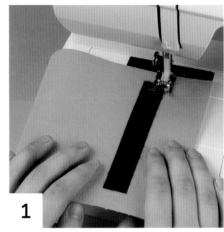

1

Sew the hook-and-loop tape.
Cut a 4½" (11.5cm)-long piece of hook-and-loop tape and sew the pieces to the bag top main fabric (I) and bag flap (L). Place the pieces about 1½" (4cm) from the end of the fabric, centering them between the long edges.

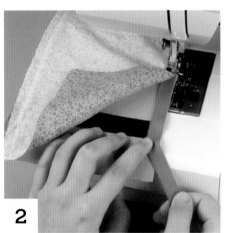

2

Install the zippers.
Install the zippers for the bag top (I) by sewing them along the long edges. Bend the zipper off the seam about 1" (2.5cm) from the end with the hook-and-loop tape so that the zipper stops at that point. Then, sew along this short edge so the top is sewn on three sides. Turn the top right side out and press.

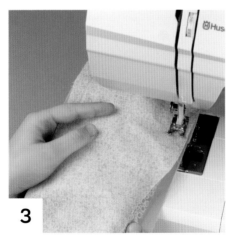

3

Create the pockets.
Create the pockets (B–E) for your desired bag according to the procedure in the Sewing Pockets feature (page 58). For the small pocket (F), however, sew the main fabric to the lining, leaving an opening in the bottom for turning. Clip the curves, turn right side out, and press. Apply the hook-and-loop tape to the pockets where the pattern indicates.

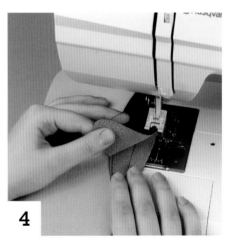

4

Apply the vinyl.
Apply the vinyl pieces (G–H) to the large and small pockets. Sew the first vinyl piece wrong side up, sewing along the edge of the pocket. Apply the second vinyl piece with right side up, sewing along the perimeter of the vinyl.

Large Bag Pockets

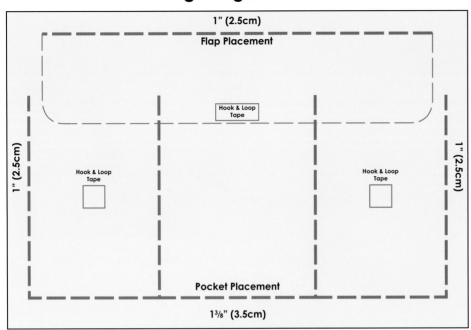

1" (2.5cm)

Flap Placement

1" (2.5cm)

1" (2.5cm)

Hook & Loop Tape

Hook & Loop Tape

Hook & Loop Tape

Pocket Placement

1⅜" (3.5cm)

Medium Bag Pockets

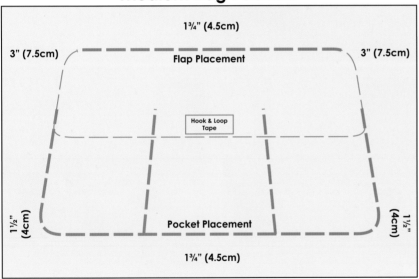

1¾" (4.5cm)

3" (7.5cm)

3" (7.5cm)

Flap Placement

Hook & Loop Tape

1½" (4cm)

1½" (4cm)

Pocket Placement

1¾" (4.5cm)

Small Bag Pockets

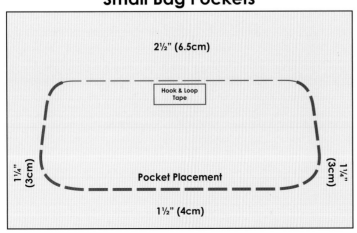

2½" (6.5cm)

Hook & Loop Tape

1¼" (3cm)

1¼" (3cm)

Pocket Placement

1½" (4cm)

Use the illustrations here for help with centering your pockets properly on the bag side (J).

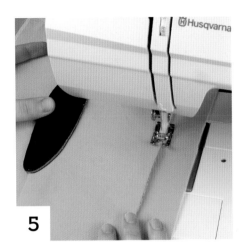

5

Apply the pockets.
Center the pockets and flaps on the bag side (J) pieces and sew them along the sides and bottom, leaving the top free. For the small pocket, apply the corresponding hook-and-loop tape to the bag side to match up with the vinyl tab.

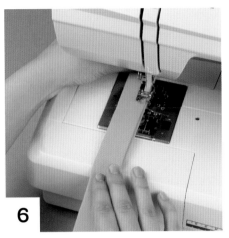

6

Make the tabs and straps.
Sew the outer tabs (N) and handles (M) following the Creating Straps feature (page 30).

7

Sew the bag sides.
Place the zipper of the bag top between the main fabric and lining pieces (J) of the bag side. Sew the three layers together and press the fabric away from the seam when finished. Repeat this for the other side.

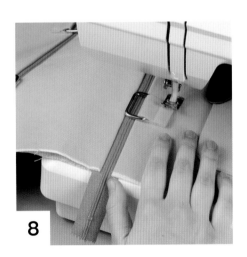

8

Apply the tabs.
Loop the outer tabs (N) through the metal rings and sew them to the bag sides with a box stitch. For the large bag, place the tabs 6" (15cm) from the bag side edge; 4½" (11.5cm) from the edge for the medium bag; and 2½" (6.5cm) from the edge for the small bag.

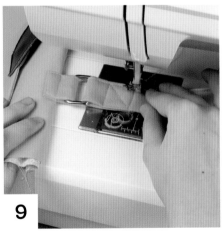

9

Attach the handles.
Loop the handles (M) through the metal rings, fold the ends over, and sew them in place with a box stitch.

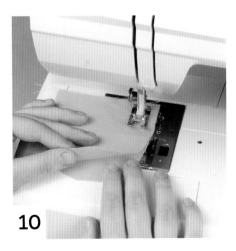

10

Sew the animal appendages.
Sew the ear, leg, and tail pieces (P–U) that correspond to your animal together along the curved edges, leaving the straight edges free for turning right side out. Notch the curves, turn them right side out, and press.

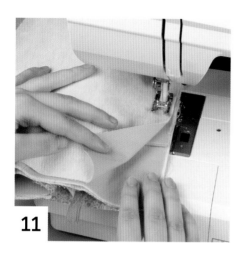

11

Sew the bag bottom.
Layer the bag bottom main fabric (K) on top of the bag side (J) with the bag bottom lining underneath. Insert the leg pieces (P) 2½" (6.5cm) from each end. Sew the layers together and press the fabric away from the seam when finished. Repeat for the other bag side with the other end of the bag bottom.

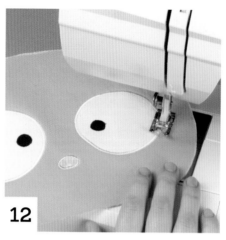

12

Stencil or appliqué.
Stencil or appliqué the face pocket piece (O) with the desired design.

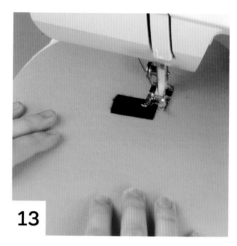

13

Apply the face pocket hook-and-loop tape.
Cut a 1½" (4cm)-long piece of hook-and-loop tape and apply it to the face pocket lining (O) and to the main bag front (A) where the pattern indicates.

14

Sew the face pocket.
Pin the face pocket main piece (O) to the lining along the upper section, stopping at the square marks indicated on the pattern. Also insert the ears (Q, S, or U) into this seam as indicated by the pattern. Notch the curves, turn the pocket right side out, and press.

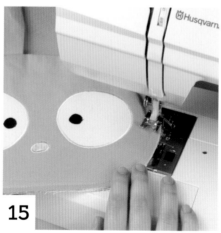

15

Baste the front pocket.
Baste the face pocket (O) to the main bag front piece (A) with the recently applied hook-and-loop tape.

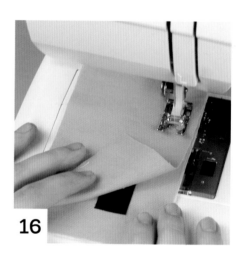

16

Sew the top flap.
Sew the sides and bottom of the flap pieces together (L), leaving the side furthest from the hook-and-loop tape open for turning right side out. Clip the corners, turn the flap, and press.

17

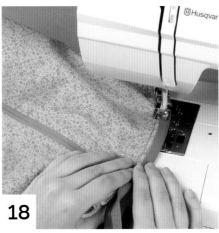

18

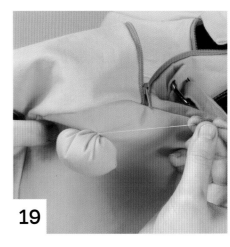

19

Sew the bag front and back.
Apply the flap (L) to the bag top (I) using the hook-and-loop tape. Fold the bag top and bottom (K) to find the center points and match these up with the center points on the bag front and back (A). Layer the lining of the bag front and back (A) with its corresponding main bag fabric, right sides facing out, and sew them to the bag sides, top, and bottom.

Bind the inner seam.
Using bias tape, bind the inner seam created by attaching the front and back.

Attach the tail.
Run a gathering stitch around perimeter of the panda or rabbit tail (R). Stuff it with batting and cinch it into a ball. For the cat tail, turn down the upper edge and stuff the tail. Hand sew either tail to the bag back (A).

CHAPTER 2: CASUAL BAGS

This set of bags is perfect for when you're on the go and don't want a lot of fuss. They can hold just a few essentials or enough to get you through a whole day, all with the right amount of flair to pull together an outfit or gather compliments from across the room. With interesting materials, like recycled t-shirts and plastic bags, and stylish details, like fabric flowers and retro motifs, these are sure to be some of your favorite bags, because they're reliable yet fun.

From left to right: Pleated Evening Bag (page 103), Styled Shoulder Bag (page 87), Expandable Retro Messenger Bag (page 97), Sling Bag (page 92)

Patchwork Purse with Side Pockets, page 82

Simple Shoulder Bag

Everyone is bound to have a mountain of unused plastic grocery bags stowed underneath the sink, or worse, in the trash. It's good to reuse them for mundane tasks, but they always seem to pile up faster than you can use them, and they never have the strength for holding anything heavier than a few groceries. Why not use up tons of grocery bags for a really good purpose, like making a strong and sturdy bag from them? The feature that follows this project shows you how to meld plastic bags together to make a sturdy, vinyl-like material. You can also create your own custom vinyl pieces from pictures, food wrappers, or other interesting media with iron-on vinyl. In both cases, you can create a simple but also very earth-friendly bag.

Smart and Simple

Playful Upcycle

All-Out Funky

With this project, it's time to let your creativity run wild, because the bag can be made using—anything! Find plastic bags in a unique color or with a quirky logo and fuse them together to make the fabric for your bag. Or take the box from your favorite cereal or the wrapper from your favorite candy bar and make your own quirky custom vinyl pieces. And there's always the option to dial it back and make this bag from standard vinyl or even fabric for an everyday piece.

Materials

- About 16 plastic retail/grocery bags OR
- 1 yd. (100cm) of 45" (114.5cm)-wide or ⅔ yd. (67cm) of 60" (152.5cm)-wide vinyl fabric OR
- 3¼ yd. (325cm) of 15" (38cm)-wide iron-on vinyl and various media
- Matching thread

Tools

- Basic sewing kit (see page 17)

Before you begin

Either melt your plastic bags following the Fusing Plastic Bags feature (page 80) or prepare the vinyl following the Laminating Media feature (page 81). Cut out the bag front and back (A), pocket (B), gusset (C), and strap (D) from the material.

Switch it up!

Instead of making your own handles, you can use purchased purse handles. Go for flexible ones that are at least 20" (51cm) long or solid ones that are 7" (18cm) wide.

See Pattern Pack for Patterns:

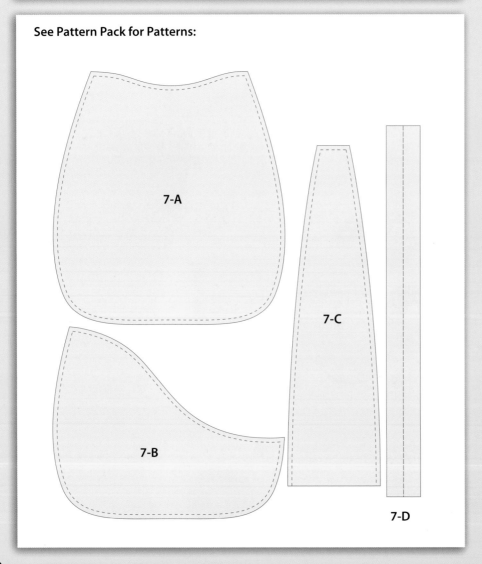

7-A

7-C

7-B

7-D

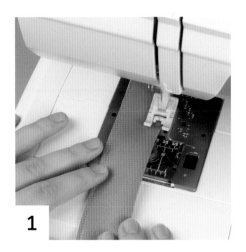

1

Sew the handle.
Fold the handle piece (D) in half lengthwise and topstitch around the perimeter.

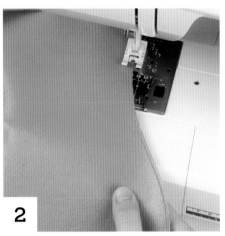

2

Topstitch the main pieces.
Topstitch along the top edge of the front and back (A) and front pocket (B) pieces. This will prevent the edges from splitting.

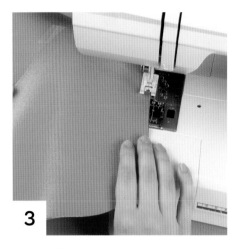

3

Baste the front pocket.
Line up the front pocket along the bottom edge of the bag front (A) with both right sides facing up. Baste the pocket in place in preparation for the next step.

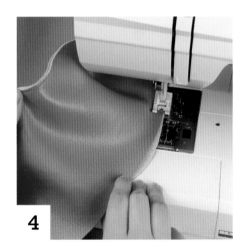

4

Sew the gusset.
With wrong sides together, sew the long edge of the gusset (C) around the sides and bottom of the bag front. Repeat this with the back and the other side of the gusset.

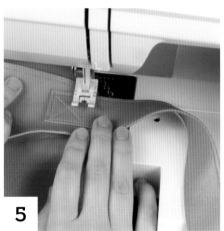

5

Attach the handle.
Sew each end of the handle (D) to the top portion of the gusset using a box stitch.

Fusing Plastic Bags into Sewable Fabric

Grocery store bags only ever seem to have one or two uses in them before they start falling apart. Why not make them more durable by fusing several bags together into a thick sheet? This sheet is then sewable, and you can use it to make any number of simply constructed bags. Bags like the Simple Shoulder Bag (page 76) and Reusable Shopping Tote (page 34) work well for this. To make one sheet, gather up about three to four grocery bags and large sheets of parchment paper. Also make sure to open your windows and get plenty of ventilation in case some unwelcome fumes start to come off the plastic.

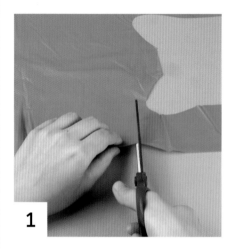

Trim the bags.
Flatten and smooth out the bags, and then trim off the handles and bottom seam. You should be left with a smooth sheet of plastic that forms a tube.

Layer the plastic between the paper.
Layer the tube of plastic between the sheets of parchment paper. If your bag has writing on it, turn it inside out so the ink doesn't melt onto the parchment paper.

Not all plastic is created equal

Each plastic bag can be different, so it helps to experiment first when ironing your bags. Use the scraps from the handles if necessary to see how your plastic reacts to different heat settings. When fusing the bags, there's a sweet spot that's the goal. The plastic should get hot enough to melt, but not so hot that it warps, shrinks, or forms holes. Experiment with different heat settings and how fast you move the iron.

When you check your fused plastic, shallow wrinkles are completely normal. However, deep wrinkles are a sign that the iron may have been too hot, so try to go cooler next time. Bubbles are a sign that the plastic didn't get hot enough to fuse completely. These can be weak points and should be ironed again.

Iron the plastic.
Using a medium-low setting on the iron and with the steam turned off, iron over the sheet of parchment paper to meld the plastic together. Run the iron smoothly and evenly over the paper for about thirty seconds until the pieces are fused.

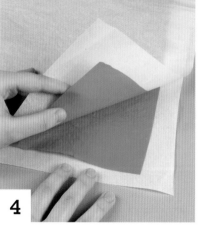

Add more plastic.
Allow the plastic to cool completely and peel the parchment paper off. Add more sheets of plastic and repeat Step 3 until you have a 6-ply sheet. An 8-ply sheet would also work well if your bags are especially thin or you want a stronger, thicker bag.

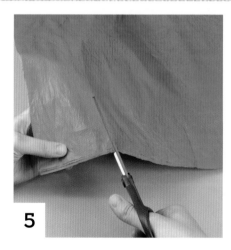

Finish and use the sheet.
After several repetitions of Step 3, you'll have a sturdy sheet of plastic that is ready to sew. You can cut it with scissors or a craft knife to the shape you need, and it won't unravel like fabric. Be sure to use a needle intended for vinyl when sewing with it.

Laminating Media with Iron-on Vinyl

In addition to melting plastic bags, you can make your own vinyl fabric from collected media and iron-on vinyl. Gather up any interesting flat media like food wrappers, photos, newspapers, or even items you've collaged yourself, and laminate them with iron-on vinyl. The result can be used to make any bag that is suitable for vinyl and faux leather—all with fabric you designed!

1

Prepare the medium.
Prepare the item you wish to laminate by making sure it is trimmed of unwanted parts and is entirely smooth, flat, and clean. Lay it on a larger piece of parchment paper.

2

Layer the sheets.
Apply the adhesive side of the iron-on vinyl to the right side of your medium. Sandwich this between two sheets of parchment paper.

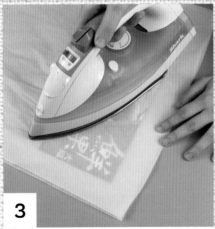

3

Iron the vinyl.
Iron the vinyl to the medium following the manufacturer's instructions. After cooling, the vinyl should be completely adhered to the medium. Repeat Steps 2–3 for the other side of the medium.

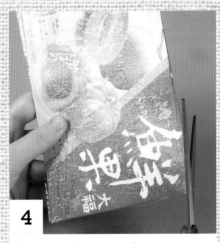

4

Prepare the piece for sewing.
Trim away the excess vinyl and use the piece to cut out your pattern. It can be cut with scissors or a craft knife and sewn with a needle suitable for vinyl or faux leather.

Patchwork Purse with Side Pockets

T-shirts are easily the most popular clothing item of this age, so it's easy to see why people can quickly stockpile a surplus of t-shirts they never wear. Why not salvage those old clothes and breathe new life into them? This bag features a fun patchwork style, but the pieces are specifically sized to fit nicely over a t-shirt design, allowing you to use up six old t-shirts while still keeping the memories in a useful application. The size is roomy, while the side pockets are perfect for holding frequently used items like a phone or keys. This bag can also be made with fabric scraps or whole yardage. No matter what, the look is simple yet stylish.

Classic Style

Coordinated Chic

Funky Upcycle

This bag is for everyone! Whether your style is chic or retro, you will love this easy-to-make everyday bag. The patchwork-style construction means you can go funky with different colors or patterns of fabric for each piece, or stylish, with coordinating colors and patterns. Alter the design further by using a fabric or leather handle, or any other handle you want! No matter how you decide to design this bag, you'll love its convenient features, including a roomy interior and large stow-and-go pockets for frequently used items.

Materials

- Six old t-shirts OR

- ¾ yd. (75cm) of 45" (114.5cm)-wide or ⅔ yd. (67cm) of 60" (152.5cm)-wide light- to medium-weight fabric

- ½ yd. (50cm) lining fabric

- 1½ yd. (150cm) light- to medium-weight interfacing

- Four 1" (2.5cm) metal rings

- Matching thread

Tools

- Basic sewing kit (see page 17)

Switch it up!

Instead of sewing your own fabric handles, you can also use purchased handles. Be sure that if they are flexible they are at least 20" (51cm) long, and if they are solid, 7" (18cm) wide.

This pattern calls for a few additional square pieces. Cut them following the chart below:

Additional Patchwork Purse Pieces

PIECE NAME	MATERIAL TO CUT	SIZE TO CUT	NUMBER TO CUT	SEAM ALLOWANCE
Tabs (E)	Main fabric and interfacing	3¼" x 3¼" (8.5 x 8.5cm)	4 of each material	⅝" (1.5cm)
Strap (F)	Main fabric and interfacing	3¼" x 21¼" (8.5 x 51.5cm)	2 of each material	⅝" (1.5cm)

See Pattern Pack for Patterns:

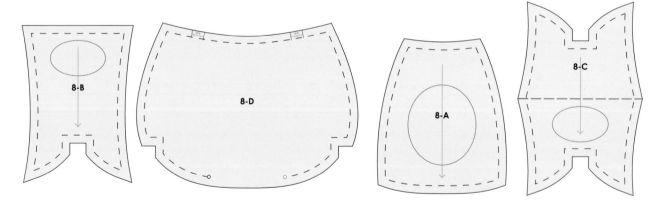

Before you begin

Cut out all the main fabric, lining, and interfacing pieces using the patterns and charts. Make any markings as indicated by the patterns. Apply the interfacing to the corresponding center panel (A), side panel (B), side pocket (C), tab (E), and strap (F) pieces.

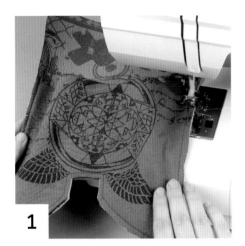

Prepare the side pockets.
Fold the side pocket pieces (C) in half and baste them to the side panels (B).

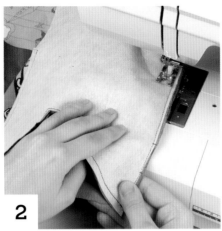

Sew the sides to the front and back.
Line up the side panel (B) to the center panel (A) along the side edge. Sew all the layers together. Repeat this with the other side of the front panel and with the back to create a ring.

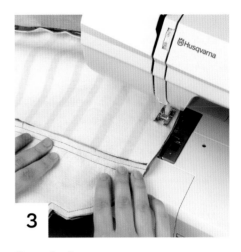

Sew the bottom seam.
Sew the bottom seam of the main bag.

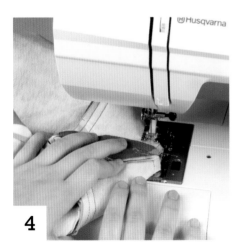

Sew the corner seams.
Match up the raw edges of the corners by folding the fabric at 45° angles. Sew along this edge.

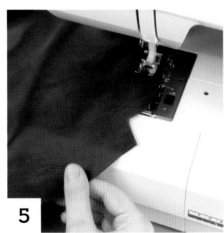

Sew the lining.
Sew the lining pieces (D) together along the sides, bottom, and corners similar to the outer bag pieces in Steps 2–4. Be sure to leave an opening at the bottom for turning right side out.

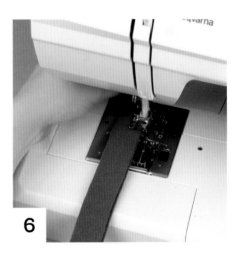

Sew the straps.
Sew the tab (E) and strap (F) pieces according to the Creating Straps feature (page 30).

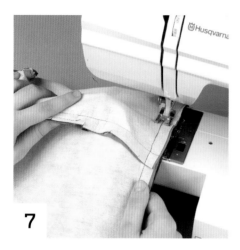

7

Sew the top.

Nestle the lining (D) into the main bag and pin the layers together. Loop the tabs around the metal rings and insert them between the layers where the pattern indicates. Sew all the layers together along this top edge. Turn the bag right side out and sew the opening closed.

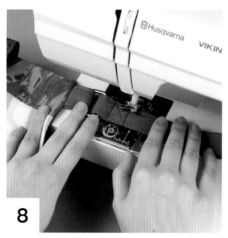

8

Attach the straps.

Loop the straps (F) through the metal rings, fold them over, and sew them in place with a box stitch.

Level: Experienced Beginner

Styled Shoulder Bag

This bag is perfect for something that you need to carry around all day. It holds enough to get you through just about anything that life has to throw at you, while the interesting shape and center panel make it look stylish despite all the work it can handle. The center panel can be swapped out with ruffled fabric, a beautiful bow, or eyelet panels for a laced look.

Classic Elegance

Summertime Style

Unique Lacing

In addition to altering the fabric used to make this bag, you can change up the look by using one of three different designs for the center panel. A ruched design creates a bag with classic style, while a ribbon adds a simple, yet special, detail. Eyelets and cording create a laced corset look that is unique and refined. And you can always choose to go super-simple by creating the bag using different colors or patterns of fabric without adding any extra embellishments.

Materials

- **For gathered version**: ⅔ yd. (67cm) lightweight fabric
- **For bow version**: 1 yd. (100cm) of 2" (5cm)-wide ribbon
- **For laced version**: 3 yd. (300cm) cording and fourteen ¼" (0.5cm) eyelets
- ¾ yd. (75cm) of 45" (114.5cm)-wide or ⅔ yd. (67cm) of 60" (152.5cm)-wide main fabric
- ½ yd. (50cm) contrast fabric
- ⅔ yd. (67cm) lining fabric
- 1½ yd. (150cm) medium-weight interfacing
- Two 1" (2.5cm) metal rings
- One 1" (2.5cm) tri-glide strap adjuster
- Magnetic snap
- Matching thread

Tools

- Basic sewing kit (see page 17)
- **For laced version**: Eyelet setting tools
- Pliers for installing magnetic snap

Switch it up!

Instead of sewing your own fabric handles, you can also use purchased handles or straps. A 20" (51cm)-long flexible handle makes this a nice handbag, while 1¼ yd. (125cm) of 1" (2.5cm)-wide webbing or strapping works for a shoulder bag.

This pattern calls for a few additional square pieces. Cut them following the chart below:

Additional Styled Shoulder Bag Pieces

PIECE NAME	MATERIAL TO CUT	SIZE TO CUT	NUMBER TO CUT	SEAM ALLOWANCE
Tabs (G)	Main fabric and interfacing	3¼" x 3¼" (8.5 x 8.5cm)	2 of each material	⅝" (1.5cm)
Strap (H)	Main fabric and interfacing	3¼" x 45" (8.5 x 114.5cm)	1 of each material	⅝" (1.5cm)

See Pattern Pack for Patterns:

Before you begin

Cut out all the main fabric, contrast fabric, lining, and interfacing pieces using the patterns and charts. Make any markings as indicated by the patterns. Apply the interfacing to the corresponding bag center panel (A), side panel (B), corset panel (C), back (E), gusset (F), tab (G), and strap (H) pieces.

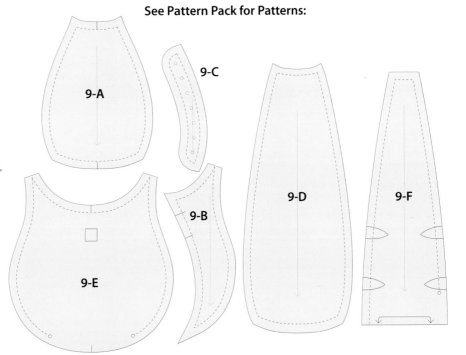

1

For the gathered version: Make the gathers.

Within the seam allowance of the gathered center panel (D), sew two rows of long stitches on either side of the center panel. Gather the fabric until it is about 11" (28cm) long.

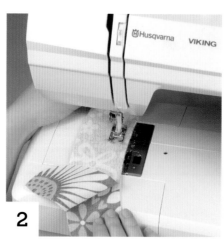

2

For the laced version: Sew the corset panels.

Sew the corset panels (C) together along the long, curved edge, leaving the shorter edge free for turning right side out. Notch the curves, turn right side out, and press.

3

For the laced version: Install the eyelets.

Using the pattern guidelines, insert eyelets in the corset panels (C) where indicated. See the Handbag Hardware section (page 20) for more help with eyelets.

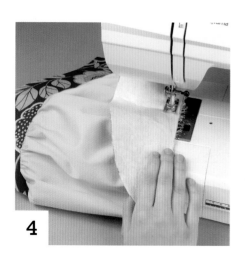

4

Sew the front.

Sew the center panel (D or A) to the side panels (B). [For the laced version: Insert the corset panels between the center and side panels while sewing the seam. For the bow version: Insert the ends of the ribbon where indicated by the pattern while sewing the seam.]

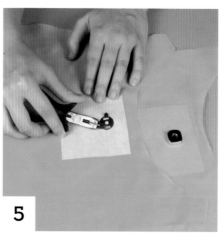

5

Apply the magnetic snaps.

Apply a rough 3" x 3" (7.5 x 7.5cm) square of interfacing to each lining piece (E). Install the magnetic snaps where the pattern indicates. See the Handbag Hardware section (page 20) for more help.

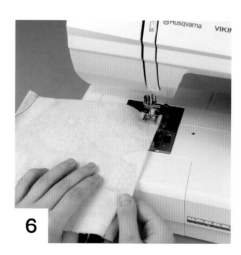

6

Sew the gusset darts.

Sew all eight darts along each side of the gusset (F). Press the darts so they lie flat.

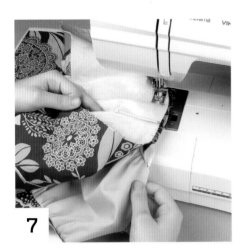

7

Sew the gusset.

With right sides together, sew the gusset along the edges of the bag front, matching up the top corners. Repeat this with the other side of the gusset and the bag back (E). Repeat steps 6–7 with the lining pieces, being sure to leave an opening where the pattern indicates for turning right side out.

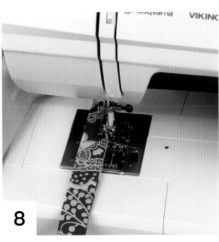

8

Sew the strap and tabs.

Sew the strap (H) and tab (G) pieces according to the Creating Straps feature (page 30).

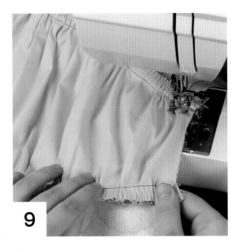

9

Sew the top of the purse.

Nestle the lining into the purse with right sides facing. Line up the top of the purse with the top of the lining. Fold the tabs (G), around metal rings, and insert them into the gusset (F) area on the side. Make sure the metal rings of the tabs point down toward the purse bottom. Sew along the top of the purse. Turn right side out and sew the opening in the lining closed.

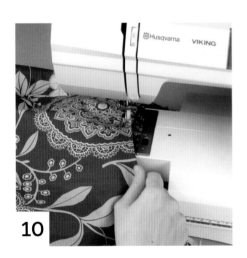

10

Topstitch the top.

Topstitch along the top of the bag, about ⅜" (1cm) from the edge, to keep the lining from peeking out.

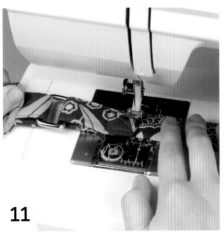

11

Attach the straps.

Attach one end of the strap (H) to the tri-glide using a box stitch. Then, loop the other end through one of the metal rings attached to the purse tabs, back through the tri-glide, and through the remaining metal ring. Secure the strap end in place with a box stitch. See the Handbag Hardware section (page 20) for more help.

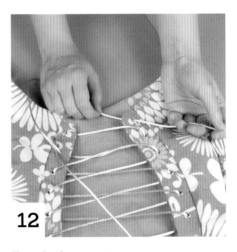

12

Finish the purse.

For the bow version, tie a bow with the attached ribbon. For the laced version, lace the length of cord through the corset panels and tie a bow.

Sling Bag

This bag is the perfect thing for hikers or anyone else who needs a hands-free bag. The chest strap makes it easy to put on and take off, and the side zipper makes accessing all of the interior pockets a breeze. Inside you'll find pockets for pens, a cell phone, a water bottle, and just about any other small but important item. And the main bag itself is roomy enough for just about anything else. The patterns for this project include designs to appliqué and stencil a number of very artistic motifs.

Sturdy and Sleek

Retro Classic

Fusion Flair

The interior and added stenciling are what make this bag a standout piece. The examples shown use solid-color fabrics for the main bag, with unique stenciled designs. To give your bag a unique look, choose a stencil design that speaks to your personality, like a floral motif, a vintage throwback, or a quirky geometric print. For the bag's lining, pick a unique print to offset the plain fabric used for the exterior.

Materials

- ¾ yd. (75cm) main bag fabric
- 1¾ yd. (175cm) interfacing
- 1 yd. (100cm) of 45" (114.5cm)-wide or ⅔ yd. (67cm) of 60" (152.5cm)-wide lining fabric
- Two 1½" (4cm) metal rings
- 1½" (4cm) tri-glide strap adjuster
- 20" (51cm)-long zipper
- 12" (30.5cm)-long zipper
- 6" (15cm) of ¾" (2cm)-wide elastic
- Matching Thread
- Stenciling or appliqué supplies & fabric (optional)

- Matching thread

Tools

- Basic sewing kit (see page 17)

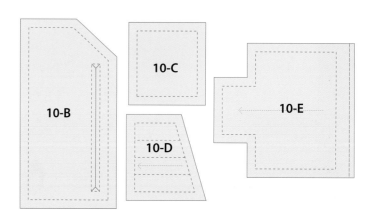

Switch it up!

Instead of sewing your own fabric strap, you can also use 1¼ yd. (125cm) of 1½" (4cm)-wide webbing.

This pattern calls for a few additional square pieces. Cut them following the chart below:

Additional Sling Bag Pieces

PIECE NAME	MATERIAL TO CUT	SIZE TO CUT	NUMBER TO CUT	SEAM ALLOWANCE
Tabs (F)	Main fabric and interfacing	4¼" x 4¼" (11 x 11cm)	2 of each material	⅝" (1.5cm)
Strap (G)	Main fabric and interfacing	4¼" x 45" (11 x 114.5cm)	1 of each material	⅝" (1.5cm)

See Pattern Pack for Patterns:

(Stencil/Appliqué designs on page 96)

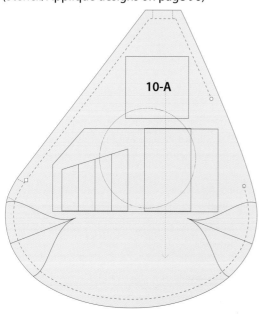

Before you begin

Cut out all the main fabric, lining, and interfacing pieces using the patterns and charts. Make any markings as indicated by the patterns. Apply the interfacing to the corresponding main bag (A), zippered pocket (B), tab (F), and strap (G) pieces.

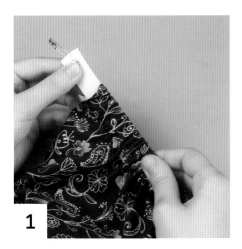

1

Prepare the pockets.
Prepare the various pockets (B–E) according to the Sewing Pockets feature (page 58). For the elasticized water bottle pocket (E), use a 6" (15cm)-long piece of elastic.

2

Apply the pockets.
Apply all the pockets to the lining of the main bag (A), following the pattern guidelines.

3

Stencil or appliqué.
Stencil or appliqué the desired design to the front of the bag (A).

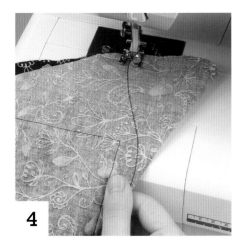

4

Sew the darts.
Fold the dart triangles in half along the fold line and sew the darts along the line marked by the pattern. Trim close to the dart and press the seam. Sew the darts in both the lining and main bag fabric pieces.

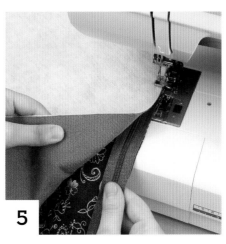

5

Install the zipper.
Pin the 20" (51cm)-long zipper to the straight edge of the main fabric for the bag front (A). Layer the lining piece under the zipper and sew the layers together, being sure to stop where the pattern indicates with a square. Press the seam away from the zipper. Repeat this with the bag back, remaining lining piece, and other side of the zipper.

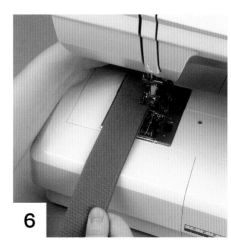

6

Sew the strap and tabs.
Sew the strap (G) and tab (F) pieces according to the Creating Straps feature (page 30).

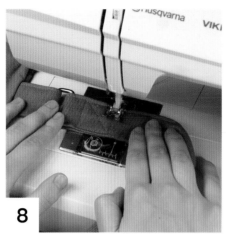

Sew the body of the bag.

Position the bag pieces so the bag front and back (A) are aligned and the bag lining pieces are aligned. Pin the two outer bag pieces together and the two lining pieces together. Fold the tab pieces (F) in half around metal rings, and insert them between the outer bag pieces where the pattern indicates. Make sure the rings attached to the tabs are pointing downward toward the bottom of the bag. Sew the layers together, making sure to sew slowly and carefully over the zipper and leave an opening in the lining for turning right side out.

Finish the bag.

Turn the bag right side out and sew the opening in the lining closed. Attach one end of the strap (G) to the tri-glide using a box stitch. Then, loop the other end through one of the metal rings of the bag, back through the tri-glide, and through the remaining metal ring. Secure the end with a box stitch. See the Handbag Hardware section (page 20) for more help.

Items for stenciling or appliqué

Copy at 400%

"Peace" Chinese Character Motif

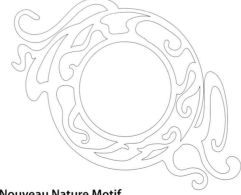

Nouveau Nature Motif

Crest Motif

Expandable Retro Messenger Bag

No wardrobe would be complete without a useful messenger bag. This bag can hold everything but the kitchen sink and is comfortable and stylish to boot. It looks great on everyone and has retro motifs for an added touch. There are a wealth of pockets on the front and an extra one in the flap of the bag. Not only that, the bag is expandable, with a side zipper that opens out the bottom by several more inches.

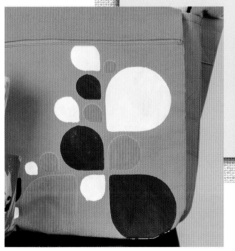

Creative Colors

Trendy Techno

Sophisticated Swirls

Get creative with this classic bag. Use custom stencil or appliqué patterns to create a design that's truly you. Use the lining of the bag as an opportunity to play with pattern or color by selecting an interesting fabric with a unique look. For an extra touch, use fabric in a different color than the exterior of the bag for the pocket pieces or for the flap.

By incorporating a zipper panel in this bag's design, you can adjust the width, giving yourself more or less room as needed!

Materials

- 1¾ yd. (175cm) of 45" (114.5cm)-wide or 1¼ yd. (125cm) of 60" (152.5cm)-wide medium-weight main fabric

- **For contrast gusset (optional):** ¼ yd. (25cm) contrast fabric

- 1½ yd. (150cm) of 45" (114.5cm)-wide or 1 yd. (100cm) of 60" (152.5cm)-wide lining fabric

- 3 yd. (300cm) medium-weight interfacing

- 10" (25.5cm) hook-and-loop tape

- 40" (101.5cm)-long zipper

- 20" (51cm)-long zipper

- Two 2" (5cm) metal rings

- 2" (5cm) tri-glide strap adjuster

- Stenciling or appliqué supplies & fabric (optional)

- Matching thread

Tools

- Basic sewing kit (see page 17)

Before you begin

Cut out all the main fabric, contrast fabric, lining, and interfacing pieces using the patterns and charts. Make any markings as indicated by the patterns. Apply the corresponding interfacing pieces to the bag front and back (A), flap top (C), flap bottom (D), gusset (H), pocket flap (G), zipper panel (I), strap (J), and tab (K) pieces.

Switch it up!

Instead of sewing your own fabric strap, you can also use 1⅔ yd. (167cm) of 2" (5cm)-wide webbing.

The messenger bag calls for a few additional square pieces. Cut them following the chart below

Additional Messenger Bag Pieces

PIECE NAME	MATERIAL TO CUT	SIZE TO CUT	NUMBER TO CUT	SEAM ALLOWANCE
Zipper Panel (I)	Main fabric	2⅜" x 42" (6 x 106.5cm)	4	⅝" (1.5cm)
	Interfacing		2	⅝" (1.5cm)
Strap (J)	Main fabric and interfacing	5¼" x 60" (13.5 x 152.5cm)	1 of each material	⅝" (1.5cm)
Tabs (K)	Main fabric and interfacing	5¼" x 5¼" (13.5 x 13.5cm)	2 of each material	⅝" (1.5cm)

See Pattern Pack for Patterns:

(Stencil/Appliqué designs on page 102)

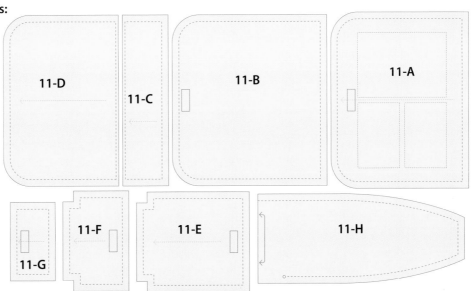

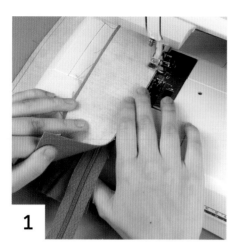

1

Sew the zipper section.
Line up the zipper panel (I) pieces above and below the zipper tape. Sew along the entire length and repeat this for the other side of the zipper tape to form the zipper panel.

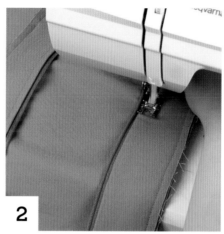

2

Baste and topstitch the zipper.
Place the zipper panel on top of the gusset, lining up the outer edges of the zipper panel with the outer edges of the gusset (H) while the zipper is open. You'll find that the zipper opens up wider at the bottom and closes at the ends. Baste along the raw edges and top stitch close to the seam sewn on the zipper tape.

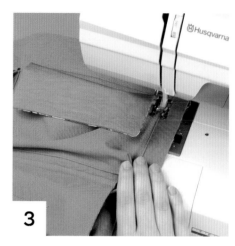

3

Prepare and apply the pockets.
Refer to the Sewing Pockets feature (page 58), and prepare and apply the deep pockets (E–F) and their corresponding flaps (G) to the bag front (A).

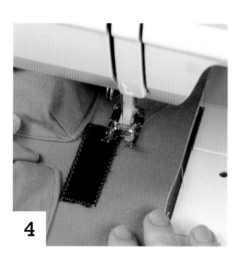

4

Apply the hook-and-loop tape.
Using the guidelines from the pattern, apply the hook-and-loop tape to the bag front (A) and flap (B) lining pieces.

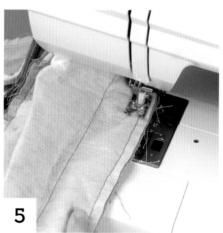

5

Sew the front to the gusset.
Line up the long edge of the gusset (H) with the sides and bottom of the bag front (A). Sew along this edge, clipping the seam allowances if necessary to get around the curves. Repeat this with the bag back. Do this same step with the lining pieces, being sure to leave an opening where it is indicated for turning right side out.

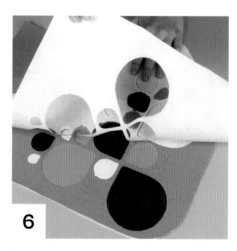

6

Stencil or appliqué.
Stencil or appliqué the desired design to the bag flap bottom (D).

Install the flap zipper.
Line up the zipper along the top of the flap bottom (D) and sandwich it with a lining piece beneath it. Sew the layers together, and repeat on the other side with the flap top piece (C).

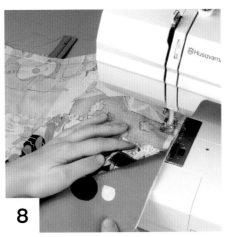

Complete the flap.
Layer the flap pieces: flap lining (B) without hook-and-loop tape (right side up), zippered flap section (C–D) (outer fabric side up), and then flap lining (B) with hook-and-loop tape (wrong side up). Pin the layers together and sew them along the bottom and sides. Leave the top open for turning right side out. Notch the curves, turn the piece right side out, and press.

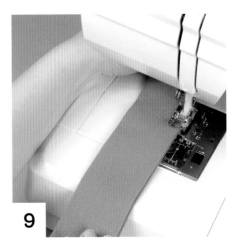

Sew the strap and tabs.
Sew the strap (J) and tab (K) pieces following the Creating Straps feature (page 30).

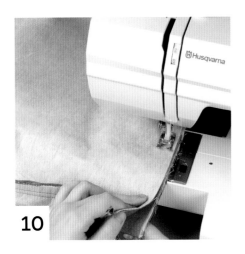

Sew the bag top.
Nestle the bag lining into the outer bag section, lining up the top raw edges. Insert the flap (B–D) between the back sections (A). Wrap the tabs (K) around the metal rings and insert them into the gusset section (H) at the sides of the bag. Make sure the bottom of the flap and metal rings of the tabs are pointing downward toward the bottom of the bag. Sew entirely along this top edge. Turn the bag right side out and press the seam. Sew the opening in the lining closed.

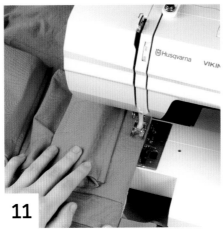

Topstitch the top.
Topstitch about ½" (1.5cm) from the top edge of the bag to prevent the lining from peeking out.

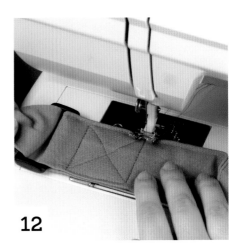

Attach the straps.
Attach one end of the strap (J) to the tri-glide using a box stitch. Then, loop the other end through one of the metal rings, back through the tri-glide, and through the remaining metal ring. Secure the end with a box stitch.

Items for stenciling or appliqué

Copy at 400%

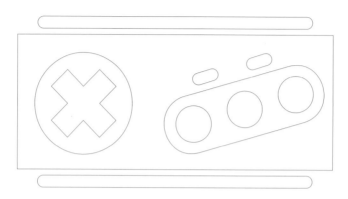

Game Controller Motif

Stripes Motif

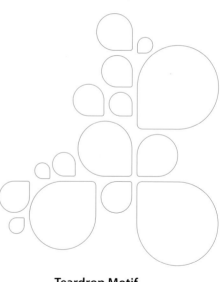

Teardrop Motif

Pleated Evening Bag

This bag is understated yet classy. With a section of sophisticated pleats and a gorgeous fabric flower, it can easily be a special occasion purse or simply one for pulling a look together. The large fabric flower is made in the Japanese style called tsumami kanzashi. It's completely removable and optional, but adds a beautiful touch. Learn how to make one in the feature following this project.

Soft Colors

Romantic Evening Bag

Everyday Fashionista

Play with different fabrics and colors to take this bag from a dreamy evening purse to an everyday fashion statement. You can even make one bag with multiple colored flowers and use the flowers to change the look of the bag. Vary the hardware you add to the flower's center to adapt your bag's appearance. Use pearls and gems for show-stopping pieces and dark metals for an everyday look.

Materials

- ½ yd. (50cm) of 45" (114.5cm)-wide or ⅓ yd. (33cm) of 60" (152.5cm)-wide medium-weight main fabric

- ¼ yd. (25cm) lining fabric

- ¾ yd. (75cm) medium-weight interfacing

- ½ yd. (50cm) lightweight contrast fabric

- 12" (30.5cm)-long zipper

- Four 1" (2.5cm) metal rings

- Matching thread

Tools

- Basic sewing kit (see page 17)

Before you begin

Cut out all the main fabric, contrast fabric, lining, and interfacing pieces using the patterns and charts. Make any markings as indicated by the patterns. Apply the corresponding interfacing pieces to the bottom (C), tab (E), and strap (F) pieces. Refrain from applying the interfacing to the bag top (B), as that comes later.

Switch it up!

Instead of sewing your own fabric handles, you can also use purchased ones. Go for flexible ones that are at least 20" (51cm) long, or solid ones that are 7" (18cm) wide.

This pattern calls for a few additional square pieces. Cut them following the chart below:

Additional Evening Bag Pieces

PIECE NAME	MATERIAL TO CUT	SIZE TO CUT	NUMBER TO CUT	SEAM ALLOWANCE
Tabs (E)	Main fabric and interfacing	3¼" x 3¼" (8.5 x 8.5cm)	4 of each material	⅝" (1.5cm)
Strap (F)	Main fabric and interfacing	3¼" x 20¼" (8.5 x 51.5cm)	2 of each material	⅝" (1.5cm)

See Pattern Pack for Patterns:

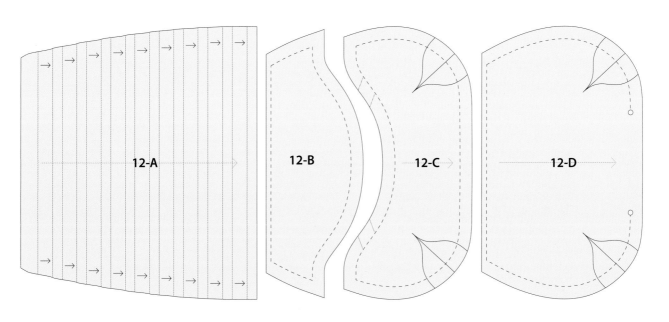

12-A 12-B 12-C 12-D

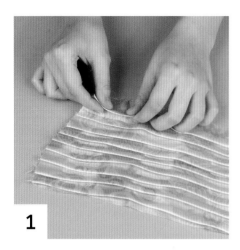

1

Pleat the contrast fabric.
Make all the folds on the pleated section (A). Fold the fabric so the lines match up to make the pleats. Hold them in place with pins or tape. Iron the pleats in place from the wrong side of the fabric.

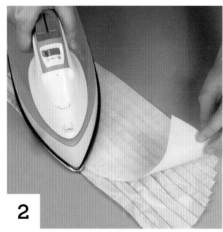

2

Apply the interfacing.
Apply the bag top interfacing (B) to the wrong side of the pleated section (A). Baste the pleats in place further by sewing within the seam allowances of the bag top template. Trim the excess fabric around the interfacing.

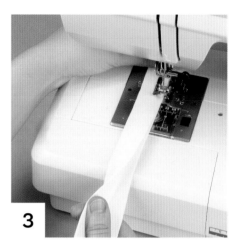

3

Sew the straps and tabs.
Sew the strap (F) and tab (E) pieces according to the Creating Straps feature (page 30).

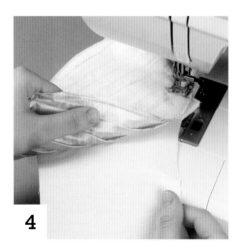

4

Sew the top to the bottom.
Pin the curved edge of the bag top (B) to the bag bottom (C), clipping the seam allowance for mobility. Loop the tabs (E) through the metal rings and insert them into the seam where the pattern indicates, making sure the metal rings are facing downward toward the bottom of the bag. The tabs will be askew so that they point upward when the bag is turned right side out. Sew the pieces together, clip the curves, and press the seam.

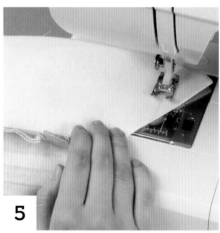

5

Sew the darts.
Fold the corners of the bag together to match up the curved lines. Sew the darts for both the bag bottom (C) and the lining pieces (D).

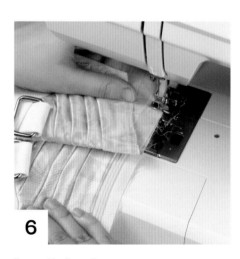

6

Install the zipper.
Line the top of the bag up with the zipper tape and layer the lining (D) beneath it. Sew all these layers together and press the fabric away from the zipper. Repeat this with the other side. See the Installing Zippers feature (page 39) for more help.

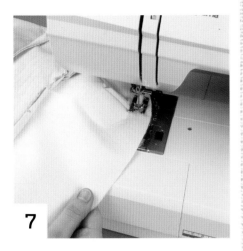

7

Sew the sides and bottom.

Match up the two lining pieces and the two outer bag pieces and sew along the entire perimeter, making sure to leave an opening in the lining for turning right side out. Notch the curves and turn the purse right side out.

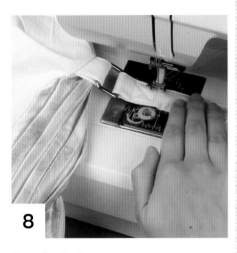

8

Finish the bag.

Sew the opening in the lining closed. Loop the handles through the metal rings and secure the ends with a box stitch. Add a fabric kanzashi flower if desired to complete the look.

How to Make *Tsumami Kanzashi*

Tsumami kanzashi are a type of Japanese hand-folded fabric flower. They are usually made as hair ornaments and have a devout following of dedicated masters of the art. The method described here is a simplified version that works nicely as a removable accessory for the Pleated Evening Bag. It can also be used as a brooch or pin for decoration anywhere. If you enjoy origami at all, you'll find that this is a very fun project and is perfect for using up a fabric stash. This method works nicely with satin fabric for soft-looking flowers, or cotton or starched fabric for crisp flowers. The look is up to you!

Materials

- ¼ yd. (25cm) lightweight fabric
- 4" x 4" (10m x 10cm) scrap of cardboard
- Beads, buttons, or other findings for the flower center
- 2" (5cm) pin back

Tools

- Tweezers
- Hot glue gun
- Craft glue (for bonding metal)

Before you begin

Cut a 3" (7.5cm) fabric square for every petal you'd like for your flower (5–7 petals is the usual). Make sure these are cut on the grain of the fabric. If you pull at the squares' corners, you should find that they stretch slightly (being the bias). Also cut a 5" (12.5cm) square of fabric for the base.

1

Prepare the base.
Cut a 4" (10cm)-diameter circle from the scrap of cardboard. Using hot glue or craft glue, cover the cardboard with the fabric and fold the edges under.

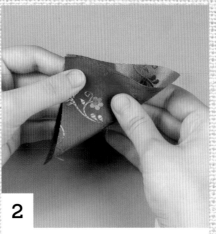

2

Fold the square in half.
Fold the square diagonally, making a triangle.

Twice the color!

For a double-colored, rounded-petal flower, cut twice as many squares, with the second half in a contrasting color. At Step 3, layer the second triangle over the first and continue as before, creating a petal with the two layered fabrics.

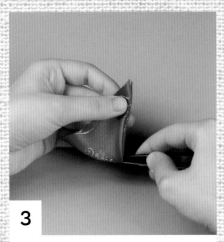

3

Fold the triangle in half.
Using the tweezers, fold the triangle in half, making a smaller triangle.

For a rounded flower petal: Fold the sides up.
Pinch the triangle at the middle with the tweezers, and with your fingers, bring the corners of the triangle up and around the middle.

4

Fold the petal in half.
Fold the triangle in half one last time to make the smallest size and the finished petal.

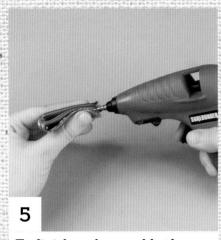

5

To finish and assemble the flower: Secure the petal end.
Place a dab of hot glue at the end of the petal to secure the ends from coming apart.

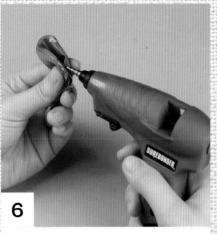

6

Secure the petal bottom.
Tuck the bottom corner of the petal inward and place a dab of hot glue to secure it. This will prevent raw edges from showing on your finished product.

7

Attach the petals to the base.
Apply a line of hot glue to the flower base and apply the petals. Repeat these steps of assembling petals until the base is filled.

8

Decorate the center.
Using craft glue, attach beads, buttons, or other findings to the middle to create the flower's center.

9

Attach the pin.
Using craft glue, attach the brooch pin to the back of the flower.

CHAPTER 3: QUIRKY BAGS

Having useful and basic bags for everyday activities is all well and good, but sometimes you want a bag that makes a statement. The purses and handbags in this chapter are perfect for people who want something eye-catching—whether it's for a child, a child at heart, or someone with a really wild sense of humor. In this chapter, you'll find bags and backpacks with crazy shapes, adorable animal motifs, and even a show-stopping piece or two. If you're willing to dive headfirst into these dazzling designs, they certainly won't disappoint!

From left to right: Reversible Creature Bag (page 116), Drawstring Bag (page 112), The Roundabout Purse (page 125), Hatbox Purse (page 130)

Reversible Creature Bag, page 116

Drawstring Bag

This bag is the perfect quick project for anyone that needs a bag in a hurry. The simple construction means that it can easily be put together in an afternoon, but the shape also lends itself well to lots of embellishment. The main section can be kept plain, decorated with downright adorable stenciling, or even dressed up to look like a squid for kids or kids at heart. The drawstrings for the top double as straps, making this perfect for light school supplies, traveling, or laundry.

Classic Flower

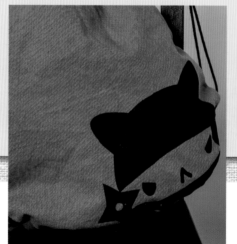

Playful Kitty

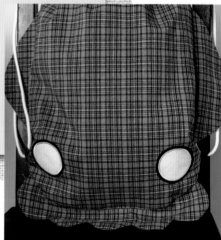

Quirky Squid

Not only is this bag super easy to sew, it's super easy to customize to your personal taste. For a classic look, consider creating a solid-color bag with a flower motif stencil and use a sophisticated fabric for the lining. You can create a more playful look by changing the stencil design to a fun character like a ninja kitty. For an all-out quirky bag, consider making the entire bag into a critter, like the squid example.

Materials

- ⅔ yd. (67cm) main fabric
- ⅔ yd. (67cm) lining fabric
- **For squid bag:** ¼ yd. (25cm) lightweight interfacing
- **For kids:** 2½ yd. (250cm) of cording, cut in half
- **For average adults:** 3 yd. (300cm) of cording, cut in half
- **For tall adults:** 3½ yd. (350cm) of cording, cut in half
- Stenciling or appliqué fabric & supplies
- About 5" (12.5cm) of ⅝" (1.5cm)-wide ribbon
- Matching thread

Tools

- Basic sewing kit (see page 17)
- Safety pin

Before you begin

Cut out all the main fabric, contrast fabric, and interfacing pieces using the patterns and charts. Make any markings as indicated by the patterns. Apply the corresponding interfacing pieces to the squid fin (B) and tentacle (C) pieces if creating the squid bag.

See Pattern Pack for Patterns:

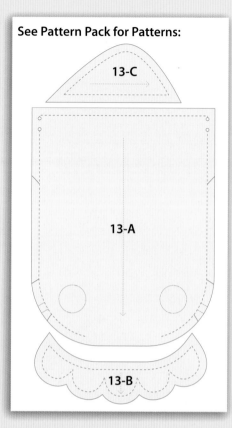

Items for stenciling or appliqué

Copy at 400%

Ninja Kitty

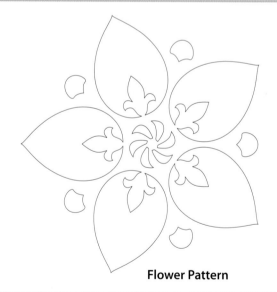

Flower Pattern

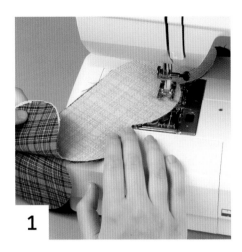

For the squid bag: Sew the squid appendages.
Sew the squid fins (C) along the curved edge and the tentacles (B) along the scalloped edge. Leave the straight edges free for turning right side out. Clip the corners and curves, turn them right side out, and press.

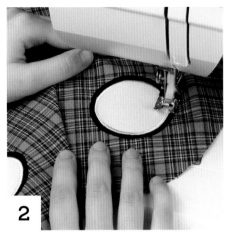

Stencil or appliqué.
Stencil or appliqué the desired design to the bag front.

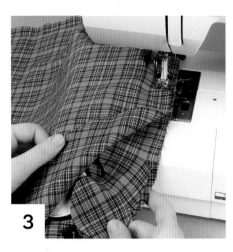

Sew the outer bag.
Cut two 2" (5cm)-long pieces from the ribbon and fold them in half. With right sides facing, pin the outer bag pieces (A) together and insert the ribbon where the pattern indicates. [For the squid: insert the fin and tentacle pieces where the pattern indicates.] Sew the layers together along the sides and bottom, leaving the top free. Leave the 7/8" (2cm) openings where the pattern indicates for the cording. Press the seam allowance open. Repeat with the lining pieces, but leave an opening for turning right side out.

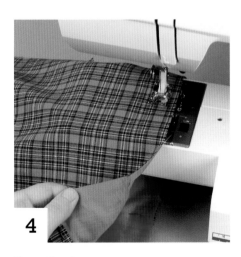

Sew the top.
With right sides facing, nestle the lining into the outer bag and sew them together along the top. Turn the bag right side out from the opening in the lining and press. Sew the opening closed.

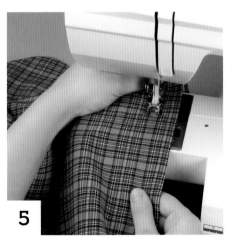

Sew the cord casing.
Topstitch 1¼" (3cm) from the edge of the top of the bag to create the cord casing.

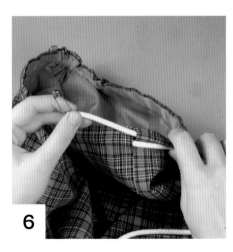

Thread the cording.
Using a safety pin, thread one half of the cording through the opening in one side of the bag. Loop it through the casing and bring it back out on the same side. Loop the cording through the ribbon at the bottom of the bag and tie or sew the cording ends together. Adjust the cording so the knot is nestled within the casing. Repeat this with the other half of the cording with the other opening.

Reversible Creature Bag

This weird bag is sure to put a smile on anyone's face. It's perfect for kids or those with a wacky sense of humor. It's just the right shape to model a number of different creatures: a robot, monster, dinosaur, and shark. With the aid of a reversible zipper, the entire bag can be turned inside out, revealing another creature as it fits your mood.

Cute Shark/Monster

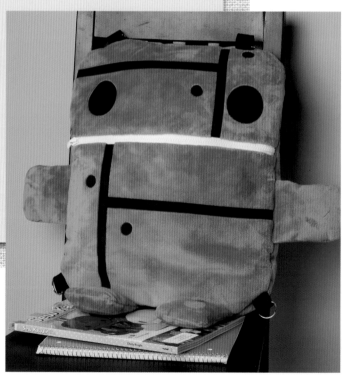

Colorful Robot/Dinosaur

With its reversible design, this project allows you to make two bags in one. This means you get to play around with two different fabrics in two different colors or patterns. For this bag, consider using a soft, snuggly fabric like fleece to make an extra-cuddly creature for a child. Bright colorful fabrics in quirky prints add to the charm of this project.

Materials

- 1 yd. (100cm) of 45" (114.5cm)-wide or ⅔ yd. (67cm) of 60" (152.5cm)-wide light- to medium-weight fabric in colors A and B

- **For dinosaur:** ¼ yd. (25cm) or 15" x 15" (38 x 38cm) remnant of contrast fabric

- **For robot:** 2½ yd. (250cm) double-fold bias tape

- 2½ yd. (225cm) lightweight interfacing

- 20" (51cm)-long reversible zipper

- Eight 1" (2.5cm) D-rings

- Four 1" (2.5cm) hook rings

- Two 1" (2.5cm) strap adjusters

- 2½ yd. (250cm) of 1" (2.5cm)-wide webbing

- Stenciling or appliqué supplies & fabric (optional)

Tools

- Basic sewing kit (see page 17)

Before you begin

Cut out all the main fabric in colors A and B, contrast fabric, and interfacing pieces using the patterns and charts. Make any markings as indicated by the patterns. Apply the corresponding interfacing pieces to the chosen character pieces: the shark and monster (A–E) or robot and dinosaur (F–K). Also apply the interfacing to the tab pieces (L).

See Pattern Pack for Patterns:

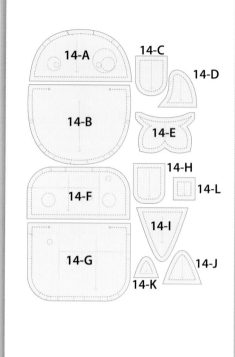

14-A · 14-C · 14-D · 14-B · 14-E · 14-H · 14-F · 14-L · 14-I · 14-G · 14-J · 14-K

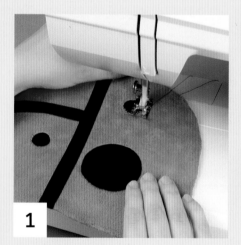

1

Stencil or appliqué.
Stencil or appliqué the desired creature designs on the Color A and Color B pieces (A, F–G). [For the robot: apply the bias tape where the pattern guidelines indicate to make the lines.]

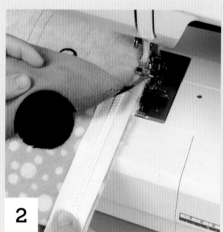

2

Install the zipper.
Center and pin the bag top (A or F) in Color A over the zipper tape. Layer the bag top in Color B underneath and sew the three layers together. Press the seam away from the zipper. Repeat the same for the other side of the zipper with the bag bottom pieces (B or G).

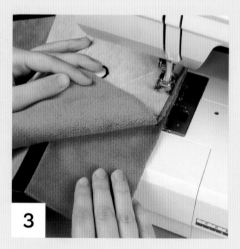

3

Sew the bag back.
Sew the bag back pieces together along the straight edge, leaving the middle open on Color B where the pattern indicates for turning right side out. Press the seam open.

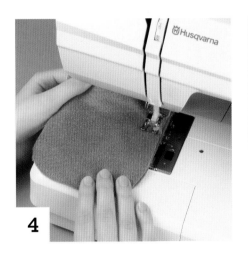

4

Sew the appendages.
Sew the various appendages for the chosen creature: arms, legs, fins, spikes, and tails (C–E or H–K). Sew around the curved edges, leaving the straight edges free for turning right side out. Notch the corners and curves, turn them right side out, and press.

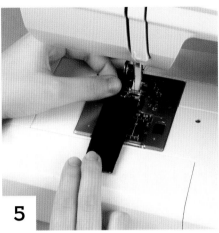

5

Sew the tabs and straps.
Sew the tab pieces (L) according to the Creating Straps feature (page 30).

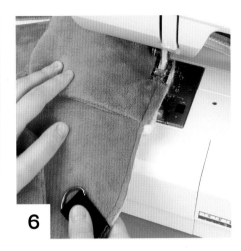

6

Baste the appendages.
Baste the creature appendages where the pattern indicates to hold them securely for the next step. Also fold each tab in half around a D-ring, and baste them where the pattern indicates.

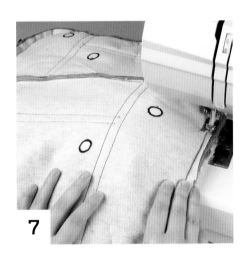

7

Sew the body of the creature.
Layer and pin together the creature's body. Layer the body back in Color A over the face of the creature in Color A with right sides facing. Layer the body back in Color B (the one with the opening) over the face of the creature in Color B with right sides facing. Sew all four layers around the entire body, being sure to sew slowly and carefully over the zipper and to move the zipper slider so it rests inside the body when the seam is sewn.

8

Create the backpack strap.
Cut a 12" (30.5cm)-long piece of webbing for the base of the strap, and a 24" (61cm)-long piece for the adjustable side. Assemble the strap with a strap adjuster. See the Handbag Hardware section (page 20) for help with this.

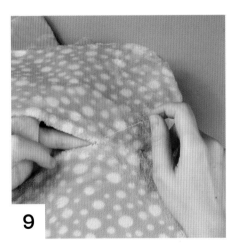

9

Finish the bag.
Turn the bag right side out and sew the opening in the back closed. Attach the hook rings through the D-rings to attach the straps.

Level: Easy

Customizable Crossbody Bag

This classic shoulder bag style purse is done up with some really cute characters. It features a handy flap with a magnetic snap, as well as two fashionable slanted pockets on the front. The overall look is understated but still adorable. You have the choice of a nerdy bunny or pirate kitty, but if you'd like something more classic, there's also a lovely flower motif.

Simple Asian Flower

Mischievous Pirate Kitty

Cute Nerdy Bunny

A bag like this is a wardrobe staple, and this one has some extra design twists, like two criss-crossing front pockets and an easy-close flap that allows for some creative stenciling or appliqué. As with all the bags in this book, a classic look is easily achieved with a tasteful color scheme and modest appliqué or stencil designs, but you always have the option to bring out your humorous side with lighthearted critter designs. For an ultra-sleek look, do not add appliqué or stenciling.

Materials

- ⅔ yd. (67cm) of 45" (114.5cm)-wide or ½ yd. (50cm) of 60" (152.5cm)-wide medium-weight main fabric

- ½ yd. (50cm) of 45" (114.5cm)-wide or ⅓ yd. (33cm) of 60" (152.5cm)-wide lining fabric

- 1 yd. (100cm) light- to medium-weight interfacing

- Two 1" (2.5cm) metal rings

- 1" (2.5cm) tri-glide strap adjuster

- Stenciling or appliqué fabric & supplies

- Matching thread

- Magnetic snap

Tools

- Basic sewing kit (see page 17)

Before you begin

Cut out all the main fabric, lining, and interfacing pieces using the patterns and charts. Make any markings as indicated by the patterns. Apply the interfacing to the corresponding main bag front and back (A), flap (B), gusset (D), ear (E or F, optional), tab (G), and strap (H) pieces.

Switch it up!

Instead of sewing your own fabric strap, you can also use 1⅔ yd. (167cm) of 1" (2.5cm)-wide webbing.

This pattern calls for a few additional square pieces. Cut them following the chart below:

Additional Crossbody Bag Pieces

PIECE NAME	MATERIAL TO CUT	SIZE TO CUT	NUMBER TO CUT	SEAM ALLOWANCE
Tabs (G)	Main fabric and interfacing	3¼" x 3¼" (8.5 x 8.5cm)	2 of each material	⅝" (1.5cm)
Strap (H)	Main fabric and interfacing	3¼" x 60" (8.5 x 152.5cm)	1 of each material	⅝" (1.5cm)

See Pattern Pack for Patterns:

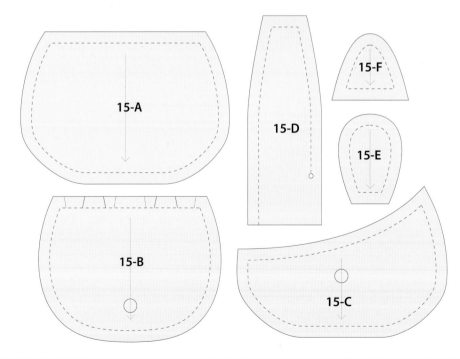

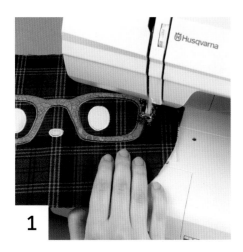

1

Stencil or appliqué.
Stencil or appliqué the desired design on the purse flap piece (B).

2

Install the magnetic snap.
Cut a rough 3" x 3" (7.5 x 7.5cm) square of interfacing and apply it to the back of one of the main fabric pocket pieces (C). Install the magnetic snap on the flap lining (B) and the pocket main fabric where it is indicated by the pattern.

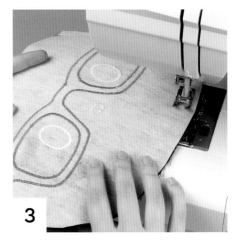

3

Sew the flap.
Sew the main bag flap piece to the corresponding lining piece (B). Sew along the bottom curved edge, leaving the top straight edge free for turning right side out. Notch the curves, turn right side out, and press.

4

Sew the pockets.
Sew the pocket pieces (C) to their corresponding lining pieces along the upper edges, resulting in two pockets that slant left and right.

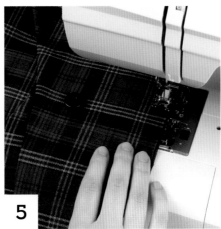

5

Baste the pockets.
Line up the pockets with the bottom of the purse front (A) and baste them within the seam allowances. Be sure to baste the pocket with the snap on top.

6

Sew the gusset.
Pin the gusset (D) along the sides and bottom of the purse front, clipping the seam allowances if necessary to match up the curves. Sew the layers together. Repeat this with the other side of the gusset and the purse back (A). Repeat this step with the lining pieces, being sure to leave an opening where the pattern indicates for turning right side out.

7

Sew the strap and tabs.
Sew the tab (G) and strap (H) pieces following the procedure from the Creating Straps feature (page 30).

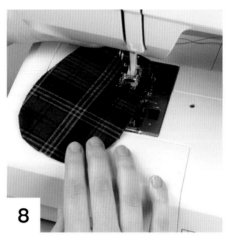

8

**For the rabbit or cat:
Sew the ears.**
Sew the ear pieces (E or F) together along the curved edges. Leave the bottom straight edge open for turning right side out. Notch the curves, turn right side out, and press.

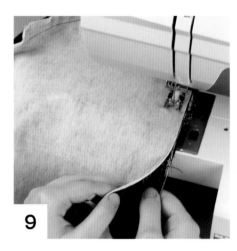

9

Sew the top.
With right sides facing, nestle the lining into the bag and line up the top edge. Pin these layers together, and then insert the tabs, looped through the metal rings, into the sides with the gusset (D). Insert the flap (B) on the back side [For rabbit or cat: insert the ears (E or F) between the flap and back piece]. Sew all of these layers together completely around the top of the bag. Turn the bag right side out through the opening in the lining. Sew the opening closed.

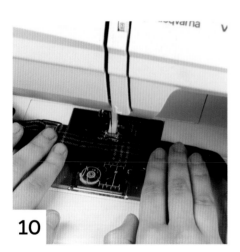

10

Finish the bag.
Attach one end of the strap to the tri-glide using a box stitch. Then, loop the other end through one of the metal rings, back through the tri-glide, and through the remaining metal ring. Sew the end in place with a box stitch.

The Roundabout Purse

This purse features a classic round shape that is sure to stand out. Despite its petite size, it's incredibly roomy and easy to access. It comes with heart, ninja star, and octopus designs that make bold and colorful statements.

Colorful and Quirky

Tough and Edgy

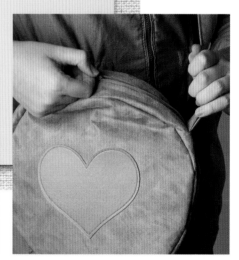

Simple and Sweet

This design takes the classic shoulder bag and makes it circular. The unique shape makes it a standout piece that you can customize. Use a sturdy fabric like denim or canvas to create a bag that will stand up to everyday wear and tear, or go with a lighter or softer fabric for a purse that you can pair with a special outfit. As always, use appliqué or stencil designs to make a bag that expresses your taste and personality.

Materials

- ¾ yd. (75cm) of 45" (114.5cm)-wide or ½ yd. (50cm) of 60" (152.5cm)-wide medium- to heavyweight main fabric

- ½ yd. (50cm) lining fabric

- 1 yd. (100cm) medium-weight interfacing

- Two 1½" (4cm) metal rings

- 1½" (4cm) tri-glide strap adjuster

- 20" (51cm)-long zipper

- 2 yd. (200cm) bias tape

- Matching thread

- Stenciling or appliqué supplies & fabric (optional)

Tools

- Basic sewing kit (see page 17)

Before you begin

Cut out all the main fabric, lining, and interfacing pieces using the patterns and charts. Make any markings as indicated by the patterns. Apply the interfacing to the corresponding main bag front and back (A), top (B), bottom (C), tabs (D), and strap (E) pieces.

Switch it up!

Instead of sewing your own fabric strap, you can also use 1⅔ yd. (167cm) of 1½" (4cm)-wide webbing.

The roundabout purse pattern calls for a few additional square pieces. Cut them following the chart below.

Additional Roundabout Purse Pieces

PIECE NAME	MATERIAL TO CUT	SIZE TO CUT	NUMBER TO CUT	SEAM ALLOWANCE
Top (B)	Main fabric, lining, and interfacing	2¼" x 14¼" (5.5 x 36cm)	2 of each material	⅝" (1.5cm)
Bottom (C)	Main fabric, lining, and interfacing	4¼" x 22¼" (11 x 56.5cm)	1 of each material	⅝" (1.5cm)
Tabs (D)	Main fabric and interfacing	4¼" x 4¼" (11 x 11cm)	2 of each material	⅝" (1.5cm)
Strap (E)	Main fabric and interfacing	4¼" x 60" (11 x 152.5cm)	1 of each material	⅝" (1.5cm)

See Pattern Pack for Patterns:

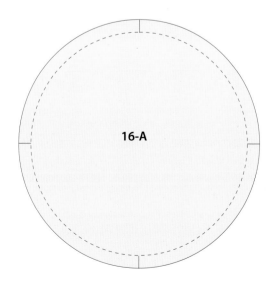

16-A

Stencil or appliqué.
Stencil or appliqué the desired design to the bag front piece (A).

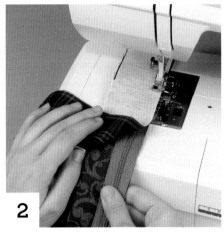

Install the zipper.
Center and layer a bag top (B) piece over the zipper and layer a lining piece beneath it. Sew the three layers together. Repeat this with the other side of the zipper and the remaining bag top pieces. See the Installing Zippers feature (page 39) for more help.

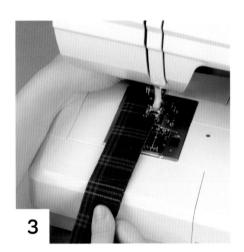

Sew the strap and tabs.
Create the strap (E) and tabs (D) according to the Creating Straps feature (page 30).

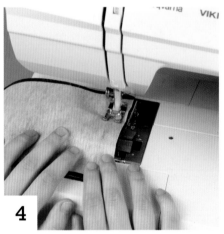

Sew the bottom.
Line up the short edge of the bottom (C) with the short edge of the top (B). Layer the lining piece beneath it and pin them together. Fold the tab piece (D) in half, wrap it around the metal ring, and insert it into the middle of the seam. Sew these layers together, being very careful when going over the zipper. Repeat this for the other side of the top, being sure to move the zipper slider toward the middle.

5

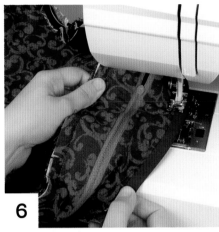

6

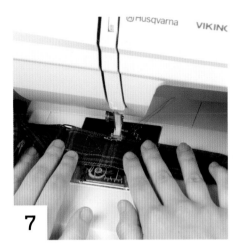

7

Sew the front and back.
Mark the cardinal points of the top (B) and bottom (C) pieces by folding them in half. Layer the front (A) with its corresponding lining piece, wrong sides together. Match up the cardinal points of the top and sides with those on the front. Clip the seam allowances if necessary and sew around the perimeter of the front. Do the same with the bag back.

Bind the seam.
Use bias tape to bind the raw seam created by sewing the front and the back.

Attach the strap.
Attach one end of the strap to the tri-glide using a box stitch. Then, loop the other end through one of the metal rings, back through the tri-glide, and through the remaining metal ring. Sew the end in place with a box stitch.

Hatbox Purse

This purse is in the adorable shape of a little hatbox. With just enough room to hold the essentials, it's perfect as a special occasion purse or to use casually. You can adorn it with several beautiful motifs included with the pattern, or even dress it up like a roll of sushi for extra fun.

Polished Evening Look

Laid-Back Everyday Piece

Kawaii-Style Standout

This purse is perfectly petite for anyone who likes to carry just the basic essentials. The small size makes it an excellent choice for an evening out, especially if created with rich fabrics and an intricate stencil or appliqué design. The purse can just as easily be made into a casual everyday item with sturdier fabric. For something to make you smile, the patterns for this bag include an adorable sushi roll design option.

Materials

- ½ yd. (50cm) of 45" (114.5cm)-wide or ⅓ yd. (33cm) of 60" (152.5cm)-wide medium- to heavyweight main fabric

- **For sushi:** ¼ yd. (25cm) white fabric

- ¼ yd. (25cm) lining fabric

- ¾ yd. (75cm) medium- to heavyweight interfacing

- 1 yd. (100cm) bias tape

- Two 1" (2.5cm) metal rings

- 1" (2.5cm) tri-glide strap adjuster

- 20" (51cm)-long zipper

- Matching thread

- Stenciling or appliqué supplies & fabric (optional)

Tools

- Basic sewing kit (see page 17)

Before you begin

Cut out all the main fabric, contrast fabric, lining, and interfacing pieces using the patterns and charts. Make any markings as indicated by the patterns. Apply the interfacing to the corresponding main bag top and bottom (A), zipper panel top (B) and bottom (C), back (D), outer tab (E), and strap (F) pieces.

Switch it up!

Instead of sewing your own fabric strap, you can also use 1⅔ yd. (167cm) of 1" (2.5cm)-wide webbing.

This pattern calls for a few additional square pieces. Cut them following the chart below:

Additional Hatbox Purse Pieces

PIECE NAME	MATERIAL TO CUT	SIZE TO CUT	NUMBER TO CUT	SEAM ALLOWANCE
Zipper Panel Top (B)	Main fabric, lining, and interfacing	2⅝" x 17¼" (6.5 x 44cm)	1 of each material	⅝" (1.5cm)
Zipper Panel Bottom (C)	Main fabric, lining, and interfacing	4⅝" x 17¼" (17.5 x 44cm)	1 of each material	⅝" (1.5cm)
Back (D)	Main fabric, lining, and interfacing	4½" x 7¼" (11.5 x 19cm)	1 of each material	⅝" (1.5cm)
Outer Tabs (E)	Main fabric and interfacing	2¼" x 3¼" (5.5 x 8.5cm)	2 of each material	⅝" (1.5cm)
Strap (F)	Main fabric and interfacing	3¼" x 60" (8.5 x 152.5cm)	1 of each material	⅝" (1.5cm)

See Pattern Pack for Patterns:

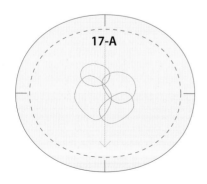

Stencil or appliqué.
Stencil or appliqué the desired design on the center of the zipper panel bottom piece (C). [For sushi: also do this with the bag top (A).]

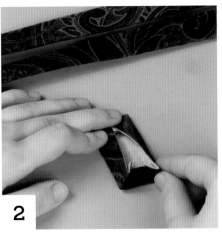

Sew the strap and tabs.
Assemble the strap (F) and outer tab (E) pieces according to the Creating Straps feature (page 30).

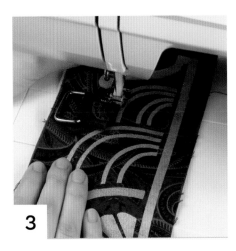

Apply the tabs.
Fold the outer tab (E) pieces in half around a metal ring and apply them 1" (2.5cm) down from the edge and 3" (7.5cm) in from the end of the zipper panel bottom (C), using a box stitch.

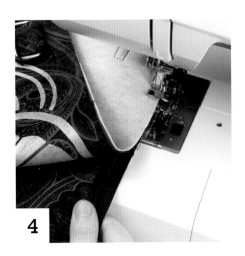

Install the zipper.
Layer the zipper panel top (B) over the zipper and layer the lining piece underneath. Sew all the layers together and press the seam away from the zipper. Repeat this for the other side of the zipper and the zipper panel bottom (C). See the Installing Zippers feature (page 39) for more help.

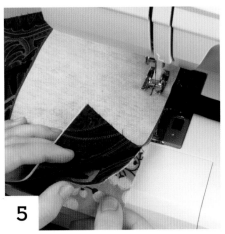

Sew the back.
Layer the short edge of the main back piece (D) over the short edge of the zipper panel, and then layer the lining piece underneath. Sew through the layers, being careful when going through the zipper. Repeat this with the other side of the zipper panel and the other end of the back piece, being sure to move the zipper slider toward the middle.

Sew the top and bottom.
Fold the zipper panel (B & C) in half to find the center top, bottom, left, and right. Layer the main bag and lining pieces for the bottom (A) with wrong sides facing. Pin them around the zipper panel with right sides facing. Match up the cardinal points of the bottom with the marks on the zipper panel. Clip the seam allowances and sew the layers together. Repeat this with the top (A).

7

Bind the seam.
Using bias tape, bind the seam for the top and the bottom.

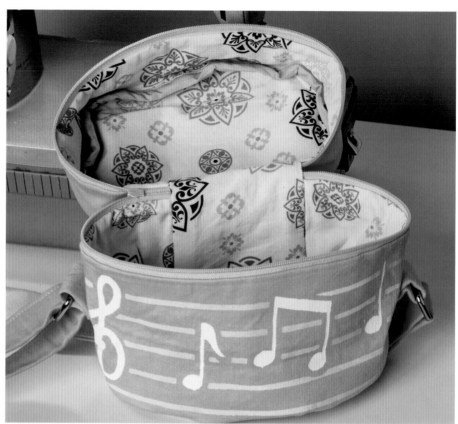

8

Attach the strap.
Attach one end of the strap to the tri-glide using a box stitch. Then, loop the other end through one of the metal rings, back through the tri-glide, and through the remaining metal ring. Sew the end in place with a box stitch. See the Handbag Hardware section (page 20) for more help.

Embellished Briefcase or Satchel

This bag brings it all together, with loads of embellishments and details that someone with a dreamy imagination will truly appreciate. Carefully tooled leather satchels and richly decorated tomes inspire the design. The bag features a strap with leather lacing and metal eyelets installed along the entire length, a twist lock, an additional handle, and a charming side pocket. It can truly take any flourishes and findings you add to it. This project may take a little more time, but it is well worth the effort to create a show-stopping piece.

Charming and Whimsical

Rich and Lustrous

Rugged and Modern

Let your imagination run wild with this project, because this bag looks great with loads of embellishments. The front flap allows for a large, detailed stencil design, while the strap allows for eyelets and leather cording. To complement the rich design, I used faux suede for the bag's exterior and a shiny, silky fabric for the lining. For a more understated look, you could choose to use more everyday fabrics. You could also use denim or faux leather with lots of metal hardware to give this bag a tough, modern touch.

Materials

- 1 yd. (100cm) of 45" (114.5cm)-wide or ⅔ yd. (67cm) of 60" (152.5cm)-wide medium- to heavyweight main fabric

- ⅔ yd. (67cm) of 45" (114.5cm)-wide or ½ yd. (50cm) of 60" (152.5cm)-wide lining fabric

- 1 yd. (100cm) heavyweight interfacing or peltex

- ⅔ yd. (67cm) medium-weight interfacing

- ¾" (2cm) metal snap

- Two 1" (2.5cm) metal rings

- Two 1¼" (3cm) D-rings

- Two 1¼" (3cm) hook rings

- Metal turn lock

- 3 yd. (300cm) leather lacing

- Forty ¼" (0.5cm) eyelets

- Matching thread

- Stenciling or appliqué supplies & fabric (optional)

Tools

- Basic sewing kit (see page 17)

- Craft knife

- Craft glue

- Eyelet setting tools

Before you begin

Cut out all the main fabric, lining, and interfacing pieces using the patterns and charts. Make any markings as indicated by the patterns. Apply the interfacing to the corresponding main bag front and back (A), bottom (B), side (C), pocket (D), pocket flap (E), flap (F), tab (G), outer tab (H), handle (I), and strap (J) pieces.

Switch it up!

Instead of sewing your own fabric strap, you can also use 1¼ yd. (125cm) of 1¼" (3cm)-wide webbing.

See Pattern Pack for Patterns:
(Stencil/Appliqué designs on page 138)

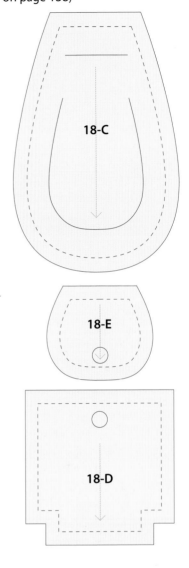

The satchel calls for a few extra square pieces. Cut them following the chart listed below.

Additional Satchel Pieces

PIECE NAME	MATERIAL TO CUT	SIZE TO CUT	NUMBER TO CUT	SEAM ALLOWANCE
Front and Back (A)	Main fabric, lining, and interfacing (peltex)	11¼" x 13¼" (28.5 x 33.5cm)	2 of each material	⅝" (1.5cm)
Bottom (B)	Main fabric, lining, and interfacing (peltex)	5¾" x 13¼" (14.5 x 33.5cm)	1 of each material	⅝" (1.5cm)
Flap (F)	Main fabric, lining, interfacing (peltex)	12¾" x 14¼" (32.5 x 36cm)	1 of each material	⅝" (1.5cm)
Tabs (G)	Main fabric and interfacing	3¾" x 3¾" (9.5 x 9.5cm)	2 of each material	⅝" (1.5cm)
Outer Tabs (H)	Main fabric and interfacing	2¼" x 3¼" (5.5 x 8.5cm)	2 of each material	⅝" (1.5cm)
Handle (I)	Main fabric and interfacing	3¼" x 16¼" (8.5 x 41.5cm)	1 of each material	⅝" (1.5cm)
Strap (J)	Main fabric and interfacing	2½" x 50" (6.5 x 127cm)	2 of each material	⅝" (1.5cm)

Items for stenciling or appliqué

Copy at 200%

Filigree Motif

Corner Motif

Starry Tree Motif

Corner Motif

Celtic Knots Motif

Corner Motif

A Note on Peltex

While any heavy interfacing will do, peltex interfacing is recommended for this project. It's an extremely stiff fusible interfacing that gives the bag a stable body. It's so thick and strong, in fact, that it's easier to work with for this project when it's cut to be about ⅛" (0.5cm) within the seam allowances. Just generously cut the seam allowances off your pattern pieces after cutting your fabric and use them again to cut the peltex.

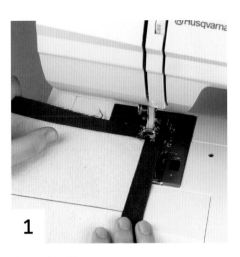

Sew the flap.
Sew the flap pieces (F) together, leaving the top edge free for turning right side out. Score the peltex (if using) 3" (7.5cm) from the top edge with a craft knife so the bag flap can move freely. Clip corners, turn right side out, and press.

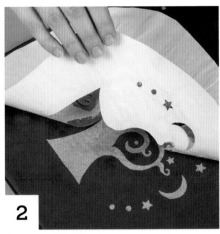

Stencil or appliqué.
Stencil or appliqué the desired design to the center of the bag flap. Position each corner motif close to the corner of the flap, and then remove the stencil and apply it to the next corner.

Install the snap.
Prepare the deep side pocket (D) and its corresponding flap (E) according to the Sewing Pockets feature (page 58). Install the metal snap pieces to the side pocket pieces following the pattern guidelines.

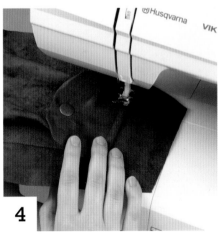

Apply the pocket.
Sew the deep pocket pieces (E & F) to the bag side (C) following the pattern guidelines.

Sew the bottom.

Sew the front and back (A) pieces to the long sides of the bottom (B), creating one long strip. Repeat this with the lining pieces, but leave a 5" (12.5cm) gap between the bottom and back seam for turning right side out.

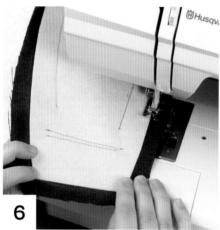

Sew the sides.

Sew the sides of the front, back, and bottom pieces (A & B) along the curved edges of the side pieces (C). Clip the seam allowances if necessary to make the piece fit. Repeat this with the lining pieces.

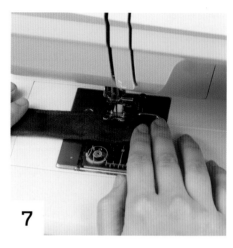

Sew the handles.

Sew the handle (I) and tabs (G) according to the Creating Straps feature (page 30). Loop the handle ends through the 1" (2.5cm) metal rings and secure them with a box stitch.

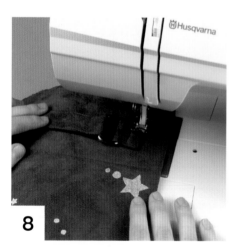

Attach the handle.

Create the outer tabs (H) according to the Creating Straps feature (page 30). Loop them through the other side of the metal rings from the handle and attach them to the bag flap (F), 1⅝" (4cm) down from the top edge and 1" (2.5cm) in from the end.

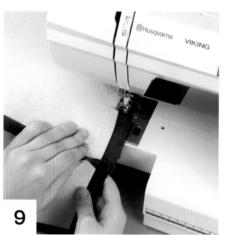

Sew the top.

With right sides facing, nestle the lining into the main bag, pinning the top edge. Insert the flap between the back pieces. Fold the tabs (G) in half and loop them around the 1¼" (3cm) D-rings. Insert the tabs between the side pieces (C). Sew entirely around this top edge.

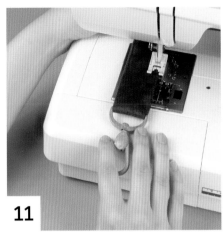

Install the turn lock.
Install the turn lock base at the center of the bag front (A), ¾" (2cm) up from the bottom seam. Install the turn lock top on the bag flap (F), lined up with the base. See the Handbag Hardware section (page 20) for more help with this.

Assemble the strap.
Join the strap pieces (J) as instructed in the Creating Straps feature (page 30). Loop the two hook rings through the fabric before making a ring with the strap pieces. As with the strap feature, fold down the long ends of the strap. Flatten the strap to make one long rectangle with a hook ring on each end, then top stitch along each side to sew the strap pieces together.

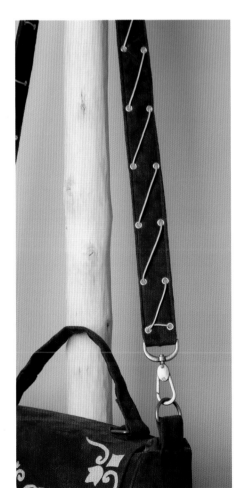

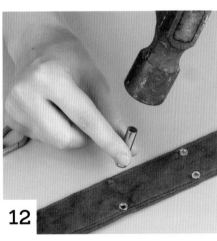

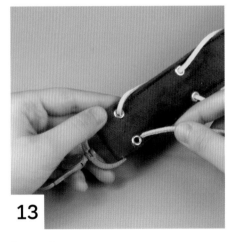

Install the eyelets.
Install eyelets every 2½" (6.5cm) along the length of the strap.

Lace the strap.
Run the leather lacing through the eyelets in your desired pattern. Use craft glue to adhere and secure the ends. The strap is now finished and can be clipped onto the D-rings of the bag.

Index

Index

Acquisition editor: **Peg Couch**

Copy editor: **Colleen Dorsey**

Cover and layout designer: **Ashley Millhouse**

Cover and bag photographer: **Scott Kriner**

Editor: **Katie Weeber**

Indexer: **Jay Kreider**

Proofreader: **Lynda Jo Runkle**

Step-by-step photographer: **Matthew McClure**

Sew Baby
ISBN 978-1-57421-421-5 **$19.99**
DO5392

Sew Kawaii!
ISBN 978-1-56523-568-7 **$19.95**

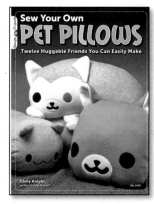

Sew Your Own Pet Pillows
ISBN 978-1-57421-343-0 **$8.99**
DO3466

Steampunk your Wardrobe
ISBN 978-1-57421-417-8 **$19.99**
DO5388

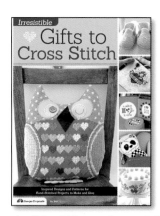

Irresistible Gifts to Cross Stitch
ISBN 978-1-57421-445-1 **$19.99**
DO5416

**Cross Stitched Cards for
Special Occasions**
ISBN 978-1-57421-376-8 **$9.99**
DO3500

Felt from the Heart
ISBN 978-1-57421-365-2 **$9.99**
DO3488

Crafty Parties for Kids
ISBN 978-1-57421-353-9 **$9.99**
DO3476

Crazy Quilt Christmas Stockings
ISBN 978-1-57421-360-7 **$8.99**
DO3483